Changes

Becoming the Best You Can Be

by

Gary R. Collins	Hank Resnik
Bill Cosby	Charlie W. Shedd
Rick Little	W. Clement Stone
Peggy Mann	Barbara Varenhorst

Edited by Hank Resnik

A joint program of

 Lions Clubs International

and

Quest International

This edition of *Changes: Becoming the Best You Can Be* is part of the revised, expanded version of the *Skills for Adolescence* program. The book is essentially the same as earlier editions except for minor changes. These include new illustrations, new photographs, and other adaptations that make the book appropriate for use in both Canada and the United States. Examples are the inclusion of metric measurements and the deletion of such phrases as "our country."

ISBN 0-933419-24-4
(Formerly ISBN 0-933419-07-4)

Skills for Adolescence and Quest International and the distinctive logos and designs associated with each are trademarks and service marks of Quest International, 537 Jones Road, P. O. 566, Granville, Ohio 43023–0566, 614/587–2800.

Dedicated
with love
to all young
people who
strive to make
the *best* of
themselves and
their world

A Book About You

This is a very special book about you. It talks about the changes, the feelings, the struggles, the surprises, the dreams, and the joys of growing up in the teenage years. You're at a point in your life when you are no longer a child. You're on the path to becoming an adult, and this means taking on a whole new set of responsibilities and making decisions you've never had to think about before. This book can help you to make the most of your life.

You may be asking yourself, "How can I really become the best I can be? What does it take to reach the top?" Well, there is no simple formula, but here are a few suggestions:

- Understand your own body and mind and what you can do to stay healthy.

- Develop a positive image of yourself to gain self-confidence.

- Learn to understand and manage your feelings.

- Build strong, meaningful friendships and stand up to negative peer pressure.

- Get along better with your family.

- Learn how to make wise decisions.

- Learn how to set and achieve goals for yourself and work hard to reach them.

Sound like a challenge? It is, and this book is designed to help you meet it with success all the way. There is a section devoted to each of the seven themes. Each one contains an article by a noted youth expert that's filled with ideas to help you cope with everyday pressures. And each section ends with a short story about teenagers dealing with the struggles that most young people face.

This is your book. It can help you to understand yourself, like yourself, and become the best you can be.

Your friends at
Lions Clubs International
and Quest International

Table of Contents

The Teen Years

Part 1

"I feel like I'm on an emotional roller coaster. Sometimes I just want to go outside and do the things that I did when I was little. And other times I just want to crawl into a hole and cry until I can't cry any more. One minute I'm acting really normal, and the next I'm yelling and taking out my anger on everyone around me. It's hard because at this age I don't know who I am, what I want to be, and what my values are."

"There are so many changes. You go from being a little kid to being an adult. You start having dances and boyfriends, things you dreamed of when you were eight years old. You have more responsibilities. Your teachers teach you new things that you aren't really ready to learn. You leave elementary school, where you had one teacher and easy homework, and find yourself with six teachers and much harder homework. There are just too many changes at one time."

"It really bothers me when adults treat you like a little kid but expect you to act like an adult. You ask them if you can do something and they say, 'You're too young.' Then if you do

something wrong, they say, 'Why are you so irresponsible?' or 'You're old enough to know better than that.' It's enough to drive you right up a wall.''

''I've grown a lot since last year, and I'm glad that now I'm not shorter than all the girls.''

You're at a time in your life when one of the few things you can be certain of is change. Changes in your body, changes in your relationships with others, changes in how you think and feel—all of these changes are happening one after another. No wonder you feel confused sometimes!

The article titled "Look What's Happening—A New Me!" was written by Bill Cosby, the well-known comedian who also has a strong interest in young people (he has five children of his own). In the article, Bill Cosby describes, with humor and insight, the many changes that people experience between the ages of 10 and 14. The main point of the article is that you're not alone, and no matter how "different" you feel, what you're experiencing is normal.

The short story for this section is called "New Clothes for School." It tells about a 12-year-old girl who returns from summer vacation to find that she's very different from most of her friends. We see in the story that sometimes the changes of adolescence can be painful and hurtful. But we also see that love and understanding can make those changes easier.

Look What's Happening— A New Me!

by
Bill Cosby

Hi, boys and girls! I'm Bill Cosby.

Wait a minute. Whoa! "Boys and girls"? That's baby stuff. You guys aren't babies. Let me start all over again.

Hi, men and women. I'm Bill...

Now, "men and women" is closer. But it's not right either. Let me try another one. Just one more. I promise. Here goes.

Hi, people between the ages of 10 and 14 who are probably in grade 6, 7, or 8! I'm Bill...

Whew! I'm having trouble just getting started. And I thought getting started would be the easy part.

Well, let's not fuss over what we call you. The fact is there's no really good label for everyone in your age group. Some sixth-graders are still very young and are more like children than adults. Others are starting to grow up. They're not adults, but they're not exactly children any more either. Some kids in grades 7 and 8 look and act like young men and women.

Whatever you call yourself (I usually just call myself "Bill"), these are the years when all kinds of exciting changes are happening in your life. That's what this book is about: changes.

The Different Changes of Early Adolescence

If you're around the age of 10 to 14 , you're at a time of life known as "early adolescence." One of the biggest changes in early adolescence is what's called a growth spurt. At this point in your life your body is either growing or about to grow faster than at any time except when you were a baby. Another word for this is "puberty." It's the time of life when human beings first become able to reproduce. They start to be like adults in many other ways.

It all happens because of chemicals called "hormones," which send messages to the different parts of your body telling them how to grow. All kinds of changes are going on in your body during adolescence. They include changes in your brain, your skin, your bones, and your muscles, for example. The shape of your body changes. Boys become stronger, girls more curvy.

But people in early adolescence don't always change the same way at the same time. Some shoot up and look as if they're going to turn into giants. When this happens, their aunts and uncles and grandparents always say one of three things:

1. "My, how you've grown! I remember when I picked you up and bounced you on my knee."
2. "I cannot get over how you've grown! I remember when I picked you up and bounced you on my knee."
3. "You certainly have shot up! You're going to be bigger than your (mother/father/brother/sister), and I remember when I used to pick (him/her) up and bounce (him/her) on my knee."

While all the uncles and aunts and grandparents are saying these things, other adolescents, of course, are still waiting to turn into giants. Or at least they're hoping to grow a little bit more and become teeny weeny giants.

5

According to scientists who study human growth, something really interesting is going on with today's adolescents. Today's adolescents (that's you) are getting bigger. The typical adolescent of today is much bigger than the typical adolescent of 100 years ago.

Why is this happening? So far no scientist has claimed that it's the result of listening to loud music and eating french fries. But don't give up hope. Actually, it's more likely to be the result of eating foods that are good for you (despite all those french fries). Also, today we have better health care than they had 100 years ago.

Another interesting thing about the changes of adolescence is that they aren't always logical. Your feet and head may reach their adult size long before the rest of you, for example. It may take your torso a while to catch up with your legs. Adolescence—especially early adolescence—can be a gangly period when you tend to bump into things. Adolescents come in all sizes and shapes. That's part of what makes adolescence one of the most interesting, surprising, and sometimes frustrating times of life.

There has probably never been an adolescent who, deep down or maybe even right up there on the surface, didn't want to be normal. The problem is that "normal" means many things among adolescents! At no other time of life are people the same age so different from each other. Adolescents whose growth spurts begin very early are normal. So are the ones whose growth spurts begin very late. The tall ones are normal; so are the short ones. Some adolescents get zits; some don't.

As if these changes weren't puzzling enough, boys and girls change at very different rates. Most girls begin to mature about two years before most boys. This can be difficult for everyone, especially the girls' parents, when the girls would rather be driving around with 16-year-olds in their cars than hanging out with kids their own age.

The Horrors and Wonders
of Adolescence

Adolescence can be the most horrible time of your life.

Like when, if you're a boy, people call your house and you answer the phone and they say, "Hello, Mrs. Cosby?" because they think it's your mother. (At some point this embarrassment will be over, of course. Your voice will drop—often cracking in the process.)

Like when, if you're a girl, no matter what happens, you just don't seem to be the right shape. And all the exercises you try with your door locked just make you tired.

Like when your parents want their "little baby" home from the school dance before it's dark outside, but the dance doesn't start until eight o'clock.

On the other hand, adolescence can be the most exciting time of your whole life. It's usually the time when:

7

You have a best friend. The two of you are so important to each other that you have to spend at least an hour on the phone together right after school telling each other all the things you forgot to tell each other coming home on the bus.

It can be a time when suddenly it seems as if the sun is setting just for you. Because of that, sunsets are more beautiful than they've ever been before.

Adolescence is a time of life when you really begin to think about who you are and who you want to be. This is normal. Try this simple exercise:

Stand in front of a full-length mirror. Say to the mirror: "Who am I? Who have I been in the past? Who will I become? What do I like or dislike about myself?"

If your mirror does not give you some very good answers within five minutes, it may be defective.

Adolescence is a time of the most incredible range of feelings. One moment you're up. The next moment you're down. You may even feel sometimes that someone or something else is in control of your feelings—not you. This gets back to all the physical changes in your body. In addition to all the other changes, adolescence is a time of great emotional change. All of these changes are normal.

Changes in School

Among the most important things about adolescence are the changes that occur in school. Suddenly you have four or five different teachers instead of one. It often seems as if every one of them expects you to do at least two hours of homework every night. You don't need to work out to get into shape. All you have to do is carry your school books around with you.

The point is that school is no longer child's play. It isn't any kind of play at all. It's hard work. For many kids, middle school and junior high school—grades 6 through 9—are a kind of invisible dividing line. Some say to themselves, "Okay, schoolwork isn't always going to be fun. But if I want to make something of myself in this world, I need an education." You don't have to be a genius to know this, and you don't have to be a genius to do well in school. You do have to work, though. Even the geniuses have to work. They just don't have to work quite as hard, and they seem to come up with more brilliant ideas than most of us.

Are you afraid of school? This may sound strange, but many people do develop such a fear over time. They begin to think that they can't do well in school, and the more they think this is so, the worse they do. Are you afraid to try? If you don't try, you won't risk failing, of course. But is that really the easy way out?

Part of the reason schoolwork may seem harder is that teachers and other adults are beginning to demand more of your mind. They expect you to think more like an adult than like a child. Scientists have found that the human brain, like the rest of the body, also goes through a growth spurt in adolescence. Your brain is actually getting larger! (Now, don't go and get a swelled head about this. It happens to everyone.)

As a result, adolescents start to think differently from younger kids. They can figure out more difficult math problems. When they really put some effort into it, they can tell better jokes. They can remember much more than young children. Also, their vocabularies become much bigger. Even so, many adolescents seem to get by with just a few words that say everything that needs to be said. These include "Wow," "Cool," "Gross," "Yuck," "Got wheels?" and "How much?"

The new levels of thinking that develop in adolescence can be a source of great excitement and creativity. All of a sudden you may find yourself thinking that you never really noticed the world before. Things may begin to make sense to you that you never understood. Like almost everything else, the way you actually think changes in adolescence.

Let's look at an example of how your thinking changes when your mind matures. Imagine that you poured some water into a short, fat glass and then poured the same amount of water into a tall, skinny glass. The level of the water would be higher in the second glass. A three-year-old might tell you that the second glass contains more water because it's higher. The more mature thinker recognizes that the amount of water is the same. The more mature thinker is capable of what we call "abstract reasoning."

The three-year-old can only tell you what he or she actually sees. In adolescence, you're able to think things out in a much more adult way than when you were a child. You can make connections between things (people, ideas, objects) just by thinking about them. This is something that a young child could never do.

If it weren't for the mental powers that develop in adolescence, we'd probably still be back in the era of the caveman. All of the great inventions of the modern world are the result of the kind of creative thinking that you can do now for the first time in your life.

The Challenges of Adolescence

Adolescence is full of changes, and it's full of challenges. It seems that every time you walk around a corner (either in school or in your own life) there's a new decision to make or a new problem to solve. Here are some of the "tasks" of adolescence that experts have identified. They're important things that you'll have to do in order to pass through the adolescent period successfully:

- Develop more grown-up relationships with people of both sexes
- Begin to become an adult man or woman
- Accept your body and learn how to respect it and care for it
- Become independent from your parents and other adults
- Begin to prepare for the work you will do after school
- Develop your own clear sense of right and wrong.

Don't panic—you don't have to accomplish all these things by next week. But they are the normal accomplishments of young people by the time they reach their late teens.

If adolescents are getting bigger these days, they're not necessarily getting smarter. One of the biggest challenges kids your age face is pressure to use alcohol, tobacco, and other drugs. That pressure is too much for too many young people. They haven't learned to say "No."

Most kids start using drugs (and it's usually something "innocent" at first, like cigarettes or beer) because they think it makes them look more grown-up or cool. Others do it because they think that everyone else is doing it. They don't want to feel left out—even though they probably don't like the taste or the smell or how drugs and alcohol make them feel.

Later in this book you'll read about drugs and alcohol. Using drugs and alcohol can be a quick way to ruin your life. As you get older, you'll probably know or hear of people whose lives

11

are being ruined by drugs and alcohol. Maybe you already know some. Once these adults were teenagers and they probably thought that smoking, drinking, and using other kinds of drugs was grown-up and cool. Sad, isn't it?

Relationships with Adults

A lot of people talk about a "generation gap" between youth and adults. They say it gets widest when young people are going through adolescence. There's some truth to this. It's normal for adolescents to want to make their own decisions and be as independent as possible. That's why parents who have been loving and helpful all your life can suddenly seem like nosy prison wardens. That's why friends your own age become so important in adolescence.

It's been said that in our society the adolescent peer group (friends your own age) has become too important. Adults and teenagers often treat each other almost as if they were enemies.

When an adult tries to boss you around, it can really get on your nerves. Of course. But I want to let you in on a little secret. Adults who don't care about kids don't take the time to yell and nag at them. If they don't care, they tend to ignore them. (Sometimes, though, families do have serious problems. This is different from yelling and nagging that parents do when they're trying to make sure their teenagers behave. Some families need help in working their problems out.)

It's important in adolescence to find adults you respect and admire. Strange as it may seem, someday you'll be an adult too. Chances are that unless you're extremely unusual you'll grow up to be a lot like some adults you know—your parents, possibly, or other people you like and admire.

That means a lot more than just getting a driver's license. It means deciding what kind of adult you want to be and taking responsibility for your life. It means gaining control over your decisions.

It means—if you can pull it off—becoming the kind of happy and healthy person you want to be.

If that's where you want to be headed, keep reading this book—and keep thinking as you read. This book can help you chart your course!

"Grant me the courage to change those things I can;

Grant me the patience to accept those things I can't change;

Grant me the wisdom to know the difference."

New Clothes for School

a short story by
Hank Resnik

Lisa felt a tap on her shoulder and turned around. It was Donnie Phillips, one of the creepiest shrimps in the class, holding out a slip of paper.

Donnie smirked at her. "Pass it to Judy," he said. Somehow he made his voice sound sarcastic just with that simple statement. He might as well have said, "Boy, what happened to you over the summer! You used to be okay, but now you're tall and ugly."

Lisa reached out and took the slip of paper.

Suddenly a voice shot out like the crack of a gun. "Lisa! Donnie! What's going on there?"

In one graceful gesture, Lisa twisted her arm in a big circle and plunked her hand down on the social studies quiz on the desk in front of her. Then she continued writing as if she'd just been getting a kink out of her arm. "Nothing, Mrs. Sikorsky," she said in a weary-sounding voice. "Tired arm."

"Get back to work," the teacher commanded. "You have ten minutes left."

Lisa finished the quiz early, but she didn't dare look at the note. Only when the bell rang and she filed out of class with the other kids did she get up the nerve to open it. The note said:

> *Judy—*
> *She's wearing purple eye shadow. And a purple skirt. And purple shoes. Gross!*   *Lynn*

From the hallway Lisa turned around to look back at Mrs. Sikorsky. It was true. Purple, purple, purple. She wasn't sure it was all that gross, though. She liked Mrs. Sikorsky, who was fairly young for a teacher, pretty, and blonde. Mrs. Sikorsky didn't have children yet; she said all the students in her social studies classes were her children. She probably meant it—at least for now, since it was just the second week of school. She'd learn.

It wasn't nice to pass notes like that, Lisa was thinking as she walked down the hall toward her science class.

Then came that little voice in the back of her mind. She'd been hearing it a lot lately, especially at school and around other kids. "Last year Lynn used to pass notes to you," the little voice said. "This year she passes them to Judy. But you and Lynn are supposed to be best friends. So much for best friends!"

"Oh shut up!" Lisa muttered. All at once she could feel her face getting as hot as if she were sunburned. She had actually

said that aloud! She couldn't believe it—she was talking to herself!

Two other girls from homeroom were passing her in the hall going the opposite way at just that moment. They were only a few steps behind her when she heard their giggles. It sounded as if a giggle bomb had gone off. Her face felt even hotter.

"You're so big," said the obnoxious little voice inside her head. "You could probably pick up the two of them and knock their silly heads together. Of course, that would make you look even more stupid than you look already."

As Lisa collapsed into her chair in the science classroom, she was surprised to realize that her heart was pounding. Hard and fast.

"Lisa! Over here! Hurry up! We don't have much time."

Lisa dragged her backpack across the front lawn of the school toward her mother's car, opened the door, and flung herself inside. As soon as she was seated she realized that Jimmy, her little brother (her half-brother, actually), had moved the seat forward again and she was all scrunched up. She groped for the handle and slid the seat back as far as it would go.

"How was school?" Lisa's mother asked as they drove off.

"Fine."

"Everything okay?"

"Uh huh."

Lisa could feel her mother turn and lean toward her even though she couldn't see it. She kept her eyes right on the road in front of her. It was a little weird, she had to admit, but lately she was getting the feeling that she couldn't look her mother in the eye. Her own mother. "It's wonderful to hear so much news about school," her mother's voice said in a half-joking tone. Lisa pretended she hadn't heard this, and for a while they drove on in silence. "I hope we'll find what you want, because I have to get back to work as quickly as I can," Lisa's mother said. "We should have gone clothes shopping during the summer. Now we'll have to rush."

"Can I get a couple of pairs of those new jeans made out of the shiny material?" Lisa asked. "They're so neat-looking. But there's only one kind that's really good. Lynn's mom says the other brand falls apart."

Her mother's response, after a thoughtful pause, took her by surprise. "How is Lynn? We haven't seen her for a while. Did she have a good summer?"

"She's okay. She went to the camp that Judy and Phyllis went to. The one where you get to ride horses every day. And she went to her grandmother's house. But that was boring."

"Uh huh."

For the first time since she'd gotten into the car, Lisa stole a glance at her mother. But now it was her mother's turn to look straight ahead. She wondered if maybe her mother knew that she'd picked up this information about Lynn by overhearing a conversation between Lynn and Judy in the hall while they were waiting for English class. She wondered if her mother had some secret way of knowing that Lynn wasn't her best friend any more, that something terrible had happened over the summer. Mainly, she'd turned into this giant that everybody laughed at and nobody liked any more.

T he mall was almost empty. Lisa knew that lots of kids came to the mall after school, but it was too early for them to be there. She felt relieved.

"How about the department store?" her mother said as they entered the main part of the mall. "They'd probably have those jeans."

Rushing ahead, Lisa called back to the mother. "No," she said. "The store next to the place with all the running and tennis clothes has them. I know it because I heard . . . some of the kids were telling me about it." The real question, she realized as she and her mother hurried along, was whether or not they would have the jeans she wanted in her size. Her great big colossal gigantic huge size, whatever it was.

She'd had a dream a few days ago, in fact, when her mother said she'd pick her up after school and take her clothes shopping. In the dream they went into a department store, and the clerk took out a huge ruler to measure her with. Then the clerk exclaimed, "This girl is so big that we don't have anything to fit her. She'll have to go to the giants' department." In the dream they'd gone home without buying any clothes at all. Then her mother had made some horrible tacky pants and tops on her sewing machine, using old rags for cloth. And when she wore the new clothes to school and walked down the hallway, all of her classmates lined up on either side in rows, laughing out loud as she passed by.

But, to her surprise, it turned out to be much less of an ordeal than Lisa had expected. Not only did they have the jeans she wanted in a size that fit her, but her mother insisted on buying several bright-colored tops that were on sale. Lisa was so happy about this unexpected surprise that she threw her arms around her mother's neck and gave her a big hug. For the first time that day she felt almost happy.

Then the clerk spoiled it. As he was wrapping the package, he smiled at Lisa's mother and said, "They sure are growing them bigger these days, aren't they?"

"Her father's tall," said Lisa's petite mother. "Her father's very tall."

The afternoon was ruined. The year was ruined.

Lisa managed to control herself until the car pulled away. Standing at the front door, she waved at her mother and forced a little smile.

The house was empty and quiet. "Allan?" Lisa called. No answer. Her older brother wasn't home from school yet, and she knew this was one of her younger brother's soccer practice days. For the time being at least, she had the house to herself.

She ran up to her room and threw herself on the bed. After lying there for several minutes and trying to make her mind a blank, she reached out for the package containing the pants and tops and slowly began to unwrap it. There they were. Giant's clothes. Clothes for the towering geek.

With a sudden violent swing of her arm she swept the clothes onto the floor. "I hate you!" she shouted. "Clothes, I hate you!" This time her tears really flowed. She didn't know how long she'd been crying, but after a while her pillow was wet from the tears, and she felt something fluffy brushing against her.

"Hi, Amanda," Lisa said to the orange cat. "You're so lucky you're small. Me, I'm like Alice in Wonderland when she grows so tall that she fills up a whole room. I wish there were some cookies I could eat that would make me start shrinking." The cat rubbed against her, purring like an outboard motor. Lisa smiled through her tears. "What do you know? I'm suffering and you demand to be petted. You're incredibly, unbelievably selfish. But I love you anyway."

Lisa was startled by what sounded like a soft knocking at her door. Then the door opened, and her half-brother Allan stuck his head in.

"I couldn't help overhearing," Allan said with his usual smile revealing a mouthful of straight white teeth, now that his braces were off. "You love me even though I'm unbelievably selfish. Thank you, thank you, thank you. The feeling is entirely mutual."

Without thinking, Lisa picked up the pillow and hurled it at him. "Ooh, you eavesdropper. You sneak!" He ducked to avoid the pillow. Then, picking it up, he advanced into the room and made a little bow before her bed.

"Excuse me, ma'am," he said, "but I believe you dropped your pillow."

Lisa grabbed the pillow and hit him over the head with it several times.

"Murder!" Allan shouted, his voice full of playful mockery. "Mayhem! The great pillow massacre!" Then, with a sudden lunge, he grabbed the pillow from her and began to pound her with it.

"I give up! I give up!" Lisa shouted through her laughter. Breathing hard, she grinned at him. He looked back at her through his tousled brown hair. With his turned-up smile, his dimpled cheeks, and his slightly oversized ears, he looked like a jaunty elf. He was 17, and she'd concluded many years earlier that, as far as she was concerned, he was the main benefit of her mother's second marriage.

Allan's smile disappeared as he examined the pillow he was still holding in his hands. "Someone," he said in an exaggeratedly serious voice, "has been crying on your pillow." He picked up one of the blouses from the floor. "And someone in here has been throwing clothes around." He sniffed the air like a comic detective. "I sink somesing iss wrong here." He smiled his great big toothy grin and stood there waiting for her to speak.

Lisa concentrated on picking invisible specks of lint from her jeans, and many minutes passed in silence.

"If you don't want to talk about it, I bet I can guess," Allan finally said.

"I bet you can't. Nobody understands what I'm going through, not even you. Mom least of all."

"Once we were people too, y'know. Officially I am still a teenager. Even though I look and act like a dashing young man."

"You're a boy!"

"Sometimes. But, as my English teacher keeps telling me, I am especially sensitive. That means girls think I'm cute and like to talk to me. Being short and cute and sensitive has its advantages."

Lisa decided to take the plunge, but she still didn't look at him. Instead she half-mumbled, "Well, being tall and . . . taller than anybody else in the class when you happen to be a girl has no advantages that I can see. Starting with your short friends not liking you any more."

For a while there was silence. She looked up, and Allan's bright blue eyes held hers in a lock. She couldn't look away if she'd wanted to.

"Last year," he said, "when I had that physical checkup before I went to be a counselor at that camp—remember? I went to Dr. Grant for the checkup. Finally, just before it was over, I asked him a question I'd been wanting to ask him for years. 'Doc,' I said. 'I want you to tell me if I'm going to grow any more. I'm one of the shortest boys in my class now, and I feel lousy about it. I keep thinking that if I'm just patient enough I'll grow some more. Will I?'"

Lisa almost stopped breathing as she waited for him to continue.

Allan smiled at the memory. "It was hard to ask him that, believe me. Even though he was our family doctor long before my dad and mom got divorced, and I really like him, I thought maybe I was going to throw up or something I was so nervous about asking him. But I figured he was the one who'd know."

"What did he say?"

"He didn't say anything at first. He took me over to this chart on the wall that showed growth patterns of adolescents. Then

22

he said, 'This is where you are, in about the tenth percentile. That means 90 percent of the boys your age will be taller than you. And you've passed your growth spurt, so you probably won't grow a lot taller. I wouldn't recommend a career in basketball.' "

Lisa was horrified. "What a terrible thing to say!"

"Not at all," Allan said. "He was being honest. He didn't want me kidding myself. Of course, I was kind of upset at first. 'I want to be normal,' I said. 'I want to be like the other guys my age.' I was really shook up. Then he put both of his hands on my shoulders and stood there looking me in the eye, and I'll never forget how he looked. It was like he was God or something talking to me. 'The world is made up of tall people, short people, white people, black people—all kinds of people,' he said. 'You are what you are. You can spend the rest of your life wanting to be something else. Or you can accept who and what you are

23

and you can go on to be a happy person who will bring love and happiness to others. You can choose for yourself.' "

For a while Lisa couldn't say anything. Then she spoke. But all she said was "Wow!"

"Yeah," said Allan. "Wow. I'll never forget it. Never." He jumped up and stood before her smiling. "That's why you see me before you today as I am. On the small side, but otherwise perfect." He beckoned to her. "Stand up."

"No!"

"Stand up!" he ordered. She stood in front of him. "Look at you, you little twerp. You aren't as tall as I am. You're a shrimp."

Lisa didn't know whether to laugh or cry. "I'm . . . I'm gigantic. The other girls think I'm a freak."

"They're probably jealous because they're even shrimpier than you are," Allan said with a mischievous chuckle. "They know that the basketball types—people who are even taller than I am—will prefer you to them."

"Oh, shut up."

"It's true. Now come on and show me how your new clothes look."

Lisa walked over and picked up the pants and tops from where they lay on the floor.

"Wait a second," she said. "I'll change in the bathroom. But it may take a while because I want to try something new with my hair to go with the pink blouse—so you can get the full glamorous effect."

She nearly danced over to the door.

Star  ters

So you're going through a lot of changes, right? Well, you can make changes into challenges and challenges into successes. Here are some points to keep in mind during this time of changes in your life:

★ Believe in yourself.

★ Try to do the best you can do—always.

★ Developing your potential in life means making healthy decisions right now.

★ Take care of your health and hygiene habits—they're an important part of who you are.

★ Your image is more than the way you look—it has a lot to do with the way you think.

★ When you take responsibility for your body, mind, feelings, and relationships, you'll have more control over your life.

★ Give yourself the chance to become the best you can be. Stay drug-free!

"To achieve all that is possible, we must attempt the impossible; to be as much as we can be, we must dream of being more."

Self-Confidence

Part 2

"I think people are shy because they don't have confidence in themselves and they're afraid of what other people think of them."

"When people won't or don't listen to me, I feel stupid and angry."

"I think people put each other down because it gives them a sense of power. They feel like they're better than someone else, so they pick on people who they think probably aren't as good-looking or popular."

"When one person puts another down, I think that it makes the first person feel good. It becomes a kind of contest. If you put someone down, the other kids might like you better because they think you're really intelligent."

27

This section is about self-confidence—and how it affects your feelings about yourself and your relationships with others. Sometimes it may seem to you that self-confidence is something magical that people are either born with or not. You may think that although everybody wants it, only the lucky ones have it. But self-confidence is something you can develop.

Rick Little has devoted his life to helping young people feel better and happier about themselves. He's an expert on building self-confidence. When he was still a teenager, Rick Little had an accident in which he was seriously injured. Because of what he learned through this experience, he started an organization called Quest International to help other young people learn to cope with the pressures and problems of growing up. The title of Rick's article, "You Can Do It if You Think You Can," clearly spells out his philosophy. As you'll see, Rick believes that no matter who you are, building self-confidence is a goal you can achieve.

The short story for this section, "A New Start," tells about two boys who almost experience a tragedy together. As a result, they learn an important lesson about the way in which a strong and self-confident attitude can make a difference to everyone who knows you.

You Can Do It
if You Think You Can

by
Rick Little

"I'll never be good enough for the team. I'm not going to try out."

"My brother and sister are always chosen for everything, and they get a lot better grades in school than me. Sometimes I think my parents really love them more than me."

"I don't like the way my braces look. I'm not going to smile again until these things come off!"

"What if I don't do well on the test? I have to get a 'B' in this class or my parents will kill me."

E ver feel this way—like you just aren't good enough to meet everybody's expectations of you? You're not alone. If you've sometimes felt unwanted or if you think maybe everybody else is better than you are, then here's some good news. There are plenty of ways you can discover your hidden talents and gifts. You can learn how to feel better about yourself—if you're ready to try.

How Would You Rate Yourself?

What would you say if I asked you to rate your self-confidence on a scale of one to ten? Would you be a super-confident "ten," a down-in-the-dumps "one," or somewhere in between?

Your answer might depend on how you're feeling at the time or what's happened to you during the day. But think about how you feel most of the time. Are you basically happy with yourself? Are you a confident person? Or are you someone who always thinks of others as being better and having more than you? One fact is certain: experts tell us that people who are self-confident do better in school, get better grades, have more friends, have a better chance of getting the kind of job they want, and are more likely to have a rewarding and fulfilling future.

Self-confidence affects our attitudes and performance. When we feel good about ourselves, we find something positive in each new experience. But when we don't feel so good about ourselves, every setback just seems to take our self-confidence down another notch.

Your attitudes, in turn, have a lot to do with your ability to succeed and be happy. Even though you can't see them, your attitudes are as much a part of you as your arms and legs. They show the world how you feel deep down about yourself and your life. And they affect the way your life is going to turn out for you.

You Can Make a Difference

In my own life I've had some tough times to deal with. Like a lot of other people, my family has had its share of problems. I had the constant feeling when I was a kid of not being good enough, of not being able to help myself and my family get through our problems. Sometimes I felt like giving up. But then I discovered a secret for myself. I found out that when I decided to stop looking at everything that was going wrong in my life (this wasn't always easy), slowly I began to feel better. I started to notice the good things. Then I began to reach out to help other people with their problems. It seemed as though the more I was willing to reach out to others, the less serious my own problems seemed.

I found as time went on that self-confidence is like a stool supported by three legs. Each one of the legs is important. Take away one of the legs, and the stool will collapse. The three legs of self-confidence are:

- **Taking responsibility**
- **Feeling skillful**
- **Feeling appreciated**

Self-confident people have all three of these legs supporting them, whether they think about it or not. Let's look at each one of these three legs of self-confidence. They can make all the difference.

You Can Be in Control

Have you ever heard comments like the following:

"Why do I keep getting into trouble? Everything always seems to go wrong for me."

"I'll never win. I'm just not a lucky person."

"I could never get a good grade in that class because the teacher doesn't like me."

I think I've said all these things at one time or another. Sometimes we say things like this when we don't want to accept responsibility for what happens to us. It's always somebody else's fault, somebody else's responsibility. So we go into situations with a feeling that we don't have any power, that we have no real control over what happens to us.

31

Of course, all of us have had times when we had little or no control over what happened to us. We can't control the weather or what time the bus arrives to take us to school or what family we're born into. But that doesn't mean we're helpless to have an impact on our lives. Far from it!

I've found that you can develop a positive attitude by looking at every part of your life and seeing the difference between those things that you can control and those things that you can't control. For example, I couldn't control the fact that my family was having problems, but I could control lots of other things:

- I could control whether I was going to give up—or try to help my family talk more openly with each other about our problems.

- I could control (sometimes) how I expressed my feelings of anger. When something bad was happening in my family, instead of yelling at my parents or getting mad, I could choose more positive ways to express myself.

If you have a positive attitude, you look for ways to solve problems that you can solve, and you let go of the things over which you have no control.

Sure, there will still be times in your life when you have problems, even when you're trying hard to have a positive attitude. Sometimes you will fail, even when you're thinking positively. Failure does exist. Everyone fails at something once in a while, but the important thing is how you react to failure. You can refuse to dwell upon your failures or your problems. Instead, you can turn your problems into possibilities.

How It Works

A few months ago I met a young girl who had been in a serious car accident. Before the accident she was popular and had lots of friends. She was a positive person. She knew exactly what she wanted in life. But then everything changed. Since the accident, she has become a different person. She has given up. She says, "There's nothing to live for."

Meeting this girl reminded me of another young girl I'd met several years ago. She too had been in a bad accident, one that changed her life by creating lasting medical problems. But there was something very different about this other girl—a sparkle, a warm smile, an attitude of confidence. After her accident she started a new program to help other people who have been injured in accidents. What was different about the second girl? She had turned her "scars into stars." She knew she couldn't control what had happened to her. But she could control how she would choose to live the rest of her life—in anger or in love.

You can develop a positive mental attitude by recognizing that there will be both good and bad in your life and then deciding to emphasize the good. When you do this, the good in your life increases. Why is this true? Because goodness attracts goodness. In a similar way, people with a positive attitude attract others to them.

Once when I described the idea of taking responsibility and having a positive attitude to a group of students, a girl named Elena came up to me after the meeting.

> "When you started to talk about responsibility, I thought of a time in my life when I didn't want to accept responsibility for anything," Elena said. "It was one of the most unhappy times of my life. I don't know why, but I just felt like I had no control over anything. Part of the problem was that I was feeling very unsure of myself. I started going around with a group of kids who were always in trouble. I guess all of us were feeling unsure of ourselves. But nobody admitted it. Some of the kids were using drugs, so naturally I had to prove how cool I was, and I used them too. I started coming home after curfew, not doing my homework, and arguing with my parents a lot. And then if they tried to talk

with me about what was wrong, I'd tell them that they didn't understand me. But I didn't feel that the kids I hung around with understood me either. Most of them just listened to music all the time and didn't talk much. I was really headed downhill until an old friend of mine visited from Toronto—we used to be best friends, but she moved away a couple of years ago. We could talk with each other about anything. I really trusted her. When my friend and I got together, she took one look at me and she said, 'Elena, what is wrong with you? You've changed so much, and I don't like it!' She really told me the truth about myself. I realized I had just stopped taking responsibility for my life. It was like I was letting that group of kids make all my important decisions. But I knew they didn't really care about me at all.''

What would you have done if you'd been in Elena's situation? How do you think you would have felt if an old friend told you some truths about yourself that you didn't want to hear?

Elena decided to take control of her life again. She realized that she needed to make some positive changes. She began by dropping her "troublemaker" friends. She worked a lot harder in school, and soon her grades had greatly improved. She joined some after-school clubs and began to meet new friends. By the time she told me this story, her whole attitude toward herself had changed. She'd decided she could accept responsibility— and make a difference in her life.

Elena showed a great deal of courage. But you don't have to "hit bottom" like Elena to turn your life around and be responsible for yourself.

Feeling Skillful

The second supporting leg of self-confidence is being good at something you do. Needing to know we do some things well doesn't mean that we have to succeed at everything we try. But it does mean that we need to know we have some special skills.

A friend of mine named Julio once told me about an important time in his life when feeling skillful made a big difference in his feelings of self-confidence. Here is his story.

Julio wasn't having one of his better days. He found out just as he was about to leave for school that his bike had a flat tire. So instead of riding to school he nearly had to run. He was in such a hurry that half of his books fell out of his backpack while he was rushing down the street, and one of them landed in a puddle. And he hadn't even gotten to school yet! Julio was feeling pretty bad when he went to his first class. But at least it was math, one of his favorite subjects. During class the teacher asked the students to figure out a difficult problem. Nobody had the correct answer. Julio was usually kind of quiet and shy, and he was startled when the teacher called on him to tell how he'd handled the problem. But, to his surprise, he was the only one in the class with the right answer. "Julio, that's really great!" the teacher said. For the rest of the day Julio felt as if he were floating on a cloud.

Have you ever had that floating-on-a-cloud feeling yourself? "Julio was the only one in the class who got the problem right," you might be saying. "He must have been really good at math. I'm not really good at anything." Again, I can tell you that the key thing is your attitude toward what you do. You may not be the very best athlete or student, but you are a worthwhile person with your own talents and skills. Maybe you're a good speller, a good baseball pitcher, or a good artist. Maybe you like to make model airplanes or play the piano. Maybe you're a really good listener and a lot of your friends talk to you about their problems. You don't have to be "the best"—just skillful.

You can become skillful at something if you work at it. It's a matter of really trying and not giving up. Did you know that Alexander Graham Bell tried hundreds of times before he finally created the telephone? Or that Abraham Lincoln was defeated several times before being elected President of the United States?

Whatever you do, whatever you're good at, knowing that you can do certain things well is a basic building block of self-confidence. Remember, no one has exactly the same gifts, skills, and ideas that you have. You are the best "you" that there is.

Feeling Appreciated

For me, the feeling of being appreciated—loved, liked, respected, listened to, accepted, and all the other good feelings that come with knowing other people really care about me—can make everything that happens in life so much better. We gain feelings of self-confidence when we feel accepted and loved.

Feeling loved from the earliest moments of childhood helps us to appreciate others, but the ability to appreciate others and feel appreciated in return is something that we can learn—we don't have to be "born with it." Appreciation is like sunshine—it brings joy to everyone who comes in contact with it. A 14-year-old boy named James told me a story that says a great deal about how important it is to feel appreciated:

James was the kind of person that most other kids admire and respect. He was a good student, a top athlete, and he even played in the school band. So nobody was surprised when James won election as president of his class. "In a way, getting elected as president of the class was the beginning of my problems," James told me. "I always thought it would be kind of a neat thing to be president. I'd feel like everybody in the school was my friend and people would like me a lot." But it didn't work out exactly the way James expected. A lot more people said hello to him now when they passed in the halls, and he was surprised to find that people he didn't even know seemed to be smiling at him a lot. But James actually felt a little lonely in the middle of all this smiling. "It was like I could have been anybody at all," he told me. "I could have been a robot with the word 'President' on my forehead, and they would have cared about me just as much." The thing that really brought this home to James was that one day he was riding his bike, and another boy his age saw him and challenged him to a race. The other boy was new to the neighborhood, so he didn't know anything about James. They spent the whole afternoon riding their bikes and just having a good time together. "At the end of the afternoon," James told me, "he said he'd see me around and it was really fun riding bikes with me because I could ride so fast. And I knew that he really meant it—he wasn't just playing up to me because I'd won an election. That made me feel really good—better than all the phony smiling in the world.''

James learned the importance of being really appreciated for who and what you are.

Part of what we all need is the feeling that no matter who we are and what we do, someone (usually our parents, but also friends and other adults) loves and accepts us—no questions asked, no criticisms, just a very basic "You're okay, and I really like you."

How often have you had that feeling? Who in your life makes you feel that way? And who do you love and accept in your life, no matter what happens? Remember that showing appreciation is like planting seeds. The more you sow, the more you'll get back in return.

You Can Make It Happen

At this point you may be thinking to yourself, "All this stuff is okay for people who are self-confident to begin with. But what about people who have never felt very skillful, appreciated, or responsible? It's not easy to change negative thoughts about yourself."

But you can! You can become self-confident. It's not some magical gift. It's not luck. Here are a few ideas to help you develop your own self-confidence:

- To build your feelings of being good at something, focus on the things that you do well and enjoy doing. Could you improve your skills in these areas by a little extra work and practice? If so, take the time. You'll feel better not just about your skills, but about yourself.

- Especially at your age, people tend to be very self-critical—always checking how they look and wishing they looked like someone else. Try focusing on your best qualities, both physical and otherwise. Focus on what's good and special about yourself, and you'll begin to like yourself a lot more.

- **Look for new ways to take responsibility.** Maybe you can create a part-time job for yourself, for example, by making up flyers announcing that you're available for baby-sitting, lawn mowing, and other services to people in your neighborhood. Volunteer for jobs and special assignments in school. Make the extra effort to be in control of what happens to you. You'll feel good about yourself, and people will respect you.

- Remember that your attitude about what you can do is one of the keys to self-confidence. **If you believe you can do something, you're on your way to great success in your life.**

Finally, one of the most important things you can do to build your confidence is to help others develop their own self-confidence too. Do this by listening to them, appreciating them, including them in your group, not laughing when other kids say mean things to them or call them names, and helping them to feel capable and responsible. You'll soon discover that by helping others to become stronger you'll feel stronger too. Give freely of praise, appreciation, respect, honesty, caring, and concern. As you share these gifts, they'll keep coming back to you. They'll help make you the person you really want to be.

The concept of a "three-legged stool of self-confidence" is adapted from Jim Fay's "three-legged table of self-esteem," described in *Discipline With Love and Logic*. Grand Junction, CO: Institute for Professional Development, 1981.

A New Start

a short story by
Hank Resnik

Walking down the street on his way home from school and looking around the neighborhood, Rico couldn't help thinking that his name was pretty funny if you thought about it. In Spanish "rico" means "rich." But Rico's family was anything but rich.

There, ahead of him, was the house where he and his family had been living for the last two months. They would probably live in it for another two years until his father finished school and they could return to their home town a day's drive south of here. It was a little better than some of the other houses on the street because at least it had a thin coat of white paint. Most of the houses, which stood on concrete blocks and looked as if they were made by the same giant cookie cutter, had never been painted.

No, there wasn't anything rich about Rico's family. But Rico felt ashamed of himself as he thought this. His father always said they were rich in family and friends, rich in knowledge, rich in their love of each other. And he was right. His father was a good, gentle man—and strong.

Back home his father had been a respected teacher in the high school, and he had won election to the school board. People said that someday he might be one of the most important Mexican-Americans in the state—a man whose own parents were farm workers. It almost made Rico dizzy to think about it, how great his father's future was. But that was why they were here in the city. For Papa's future.

41

As Rico was nearing his house, three boys his own age rode past him on bicycles. They were Jose, who lived right across the street from Rico, and two other kids from the neighborhood, Manuel and Angel. The boys stopped just ahead of Rico and blocked the sidewalk with their bikes. Sitting in the middle on his new dirt bike, Jose wore black jeans, shiny black boots, and a black leather jacket like a motorcycle jacket. Jose was only 12 years old, but he was big for his age. He had slick black hair and clear olive skin. At least once a week he was in trouble with the truant officer or the police.

"Hey, Rico!" Jose called. "It looks like we're in your way." Jose's voice was heavy with sarcasm. "I'm so sorry."

Rico walked out into the street to get around the bicycles. He looked Jose straight in the eye but didn't say a word.

Jose turned on his bicycle seat and called after him. "Rico, you got a problem. You got a serious problem. You talk too

much." Rico had never said more than a few words to Jose.

Rico mounted the front steps of his house, walked slowly across the porch, opened the front door, and went inside. He never said anything, and he never looked back. But he knew he would have to do something about the situation soon. It was getting worse all the time.

Later that afternoon there was still about an hour of daylight left when Rico and his little brother Pepe climbed through the opening in a fence leading onto the vacant lot they called "the field." A block away from Rico's house, this was where all the neighborhood kids played. It wasn't much of a field, though. Actually it was just a big flat place where the housing department had torn down a row of old buildings. For now it belonged to the kids. Rico was glad to see that they had the field to themselves.

"Let's do pop-ups," Rico said. "Get ready. Here it comes." Pepe ran out into the middle of the field, looking up toward the sky, and caught the ball right in the middle of his mitt.

"All right!" Rico yelled. He used the same kind voice his father used with him when they played catch together. "Now you pop me one."

The younger boy hurled the softball wildly, and it went rolling off into a clump of weeds. Rico chased after it. "I'm sorry," Pepe said.

"It's okay. You're getting better. Just try to put your whole body into it."

Without breaking his stride, Rico scooped up the ball, dropped it into his glove, and turned to throw another one to Pepe. Then he stopped dead. Jose, Manuel, and Angel were standing just inside the fence opening.

Even from across the field Jose sounded mean and sarcastic. "Lookin' like a champion, Rico. Let's see ya do your stuff."

"Go for it," Rico shouted to Pepe. Pepe ran after the ball but missed it.

"Aw, too bad," Jose said loudly.

"Throw it to me," Rico called. "Throw me a low one."

After catching Pepe's ball, Rico saw out of the corner of his eye that Jose was moving toward him. The two other boys remained at the fence opening, blocking it. That was the only way out from the field.

"Rico, we gotta talk," Jose said in a mean voice as he came closer. "We don't talk enough, you and me. If you talked to me, I might not want to beat you up."

"Talk to him, Rico," Pepe shouted from across the field. "Talk to him!" Rico could hear the fear in Pepe's voice.

"It's okay," he called. "I'll be all right."

"Sure," Jose said. "He'll be just fine. After I'm done with him, he won't be feeling a thing." By now Jose was standing so close that Rico could feel his breath. Jose was taller than Rico.

Rico's whole body was shaking. He looked Jose straight in the eye. "I'm not afraid of you," he said.

Jose looked at the ground for a moment as if he were thinking. Then suddenly he flipped his head up and said, "Well, we gotta do something about that, don't we?" Before Rico knew what was happening, Jose had grabbed his shirt by the collar, squeezed it tight, and pulled him forward. "We just gotta do something about that." Jose drew his arm back, and his hand was a hard fist.

Rico ducked just as Jose swung. In the same motion Rico moved forward, leading with his head, into Jose's stomach. Jose let out a yelp of surprise. Then, before Jose had time to rally, Rico dove for his ankles. In a moment Jose was lying flat on the ground on his back, and Rico was on top of him, pinning his shoulders.

Jose struggled to fight his way out of the hold Rico had on him. But this hold had worked for Rico several times in the past. His father had taught it to him after learning it in the Army. Rico knew how to take down a grown man if he needed to.

"I don't want to hurt you," Rico said, "but I can hurt you if I have to."

Jose struggled some more but couldn't move. He looked up at Rico, his coal eyes blazing.

The fight had lasted less than a minute, but Rico knew it was over. He stood up, brushed the dirt off his hands, and reached for his mitt lying on the ground. Now he felt very calm. "No hard feelings, Jose. You guys want to play catch with me and my brother?"

Jose dusted off his jacket and pants as he stood up. "You're such a good boy," he said. "Everybody likes you. But me, you make me sick. I won't forget this. You watch out."

Rico said nothing. He stood watching until Jose, Manuel, and Angel disappeared through the opening in the fence.

Later that evening the whole family said their prayers together, as usual. It was a nice family time. After prayers everybody got a chance to share something about the day that was ending. "Pepe, why are you so quiet tonight?" Papa asked at one point. "Nothing happened to you today?"

"Rico may not be so big, but he's strong," Pepe blurted out. Then he looked quickly toward his brother.

"That's very interesting," Papa said. "Anything else?"

"No, Papa, I promised Rico I wouldn't tell."

Everyone looked at Rico—Mama, Papa, Pepe, Elida, Carmen, and Rita—waiting for him to speak.

"Jose tried to beat me up," Rico finally said with a sigh. "So I pinned him on the ground. It was no big deal."

"Oooh, I don't like that boy!" Mama said. "He's a bad boy. Trouble."

"I'm not sure about that," said Papa. "He has some problems."

"Yes," said Mama. "His mama is very sick. That's not his fault."

"His mama drinks too much," offered Elida, the oldest girl. "Once I smelled one of the bottles she threw out. Phew!"

Pepe couldn't contain his excitement. "Do you think he really carries a knife?" he asked. "Rico said Jose will use a knife on him next time. Jose hates his guts."

"Enough of this," Papa said. "People who worry never get anything done. If anything happens, Jose will be hearing from me. Now everybody to bed. Time for kisses and hugs."

Several days went by, but Rico saw nothing of Jose and the others. Jose didn't even come to school. Mama said that Jose and his mama were both very sick. Rico almost forgot about him.

Late one night about a week after the fight with Jose at the field, Rico was awakened by a strange stinging smell. His bed was right next to a window at the front of the house overlooking the street. The window was open, and the smell was coming in from the street.

Rico sat up in bed, rubbing the sleep out of his eyes, then pulled the curtain and looked out. Clouds of thick, black smoke were pouring out of the house where Jose and his mother lived. Then Rico saw orange flames inside what must have been the living room.

Rico jumped out of bed, switched on the overhead light near the door, grabbed his sneakers, and started to put them on. "Pepe!" he shouted. "Go wake up Mama and Papa. There's a fire! Hurry!"

"Whaa . . .?" Pepe mumbled.

"Get up!" Rico shouted. "Wake Mama and Papa! I'm going across the street." Then, remembering something he'd read in his Boy Scout book about what to do in a fire, he grabbed his towel from the hook next to the bedroom door and ran out.

By the time he reached the front of Jose's house, flames were jumping out from the roof. Rico stood on the sidewalk wondering what to do.

Then he heard a moaning sound inside the house. The moans turned to screams. Rico watched in terror as a shape like a ghost plunged through the front door and nearly flew across the porch and onto the sidewalk. The shape turned out to be an old woman with gray hair, dressed in a shabby bathrobe and torn pajamas. As she ran, the woman called out in a hoarse voice, "Jose! Jose! My son!" She looked more dead than alive.

Now Rico knew what he had to do. Without waiting any longer, he covered his face with his towel and rushed inside.

The smoke was thick and black. As soon as he was inside the front door, his eyes began to water from the pain. The house was a lot like his own house inside, only shabbier. He rushed forward to where in his own house there was a door to the small front bedroom. Sure enough, the door was there. But the room was empty except for an old metal bed frame and springs.

The second bedroom, down the hall, was filled with smoke, and Rico could hardly see what was in it. He could just make out the shape of a bed, and he leaped across to see what was there.

His free hand touched a boy's body. Jose. Rico stooped over, picked up the body, and frantically began to pull it along the floor. As he did this, the towel fell from his face, and he began to choke on the thick, black smoke that filled the room.

Seeing that the flames now filled the front of the house, Rico knew that he would have to go out the back door. "I pray,"

Rico said to himself, "that it's as much like our house as it's been so far. I pray for the back door to be there like in our house." Pulling the body, he lurched toward where the kitchen would be.

Rico found the kitchen, but the door leading outside was not where it should have been. The kitchen was also filled with smoke, and he groped along the walls, hoping to find a window. Finally his free hand told him he'd found a doorknob. In a second he was outside.

He gasped for fresh air. It was like coming up from the bottom of an ocean after starting to drown.

Then he dragged the body out to the street in front of the house. It seemed that all of the neighbors and half the firemen in the city were there.

"Rico! Rico!" Mama screamed as she rushed over to him. He dropped the body to the ground and fell, exhausted, into her arms.

Nearly two weeks had passed since the night of the fire. It was one of those warm evenings with a full moon. Rico couldn't sleep. The window next to his bed was wide open, and a gentle breeze lifted the curtains every now and then.

Lying on his side and looking out at the moonlit street, Rico thought about the events of two weeks ago, when Jose's house had nearly burned down. Now he could see clearly across the street where Jose's older brother, with the help of many of the neighbors, had started to rebuild the old cottage. Jose's brother had come from another town and taken his mother to a special rest home. Everyone knew it was a place for people who get sick from too much drinking. But everyone said that at least Jose and his mother were alive.

Rico gazed across the street and remembered the smoke, the fire, and the sounds of the fire engines and people screaming.

"It's nice out, huh?" said a voice from the next bed.

"You awake, Jose?" Rico said.

"It's too hot to sleep."

"Yeah. I think I'm gonna go outside for a while." Rico reached for his shoes and a pair of shorts. Now with the cot for Jose, there was hardly enough room to open the door. But it wouldn't be for long. Soon Jose's mama would come back home and they'd be able to live in their own house again. Papa had insisted that Jose stay with them until the house was ready and Jose's mama was better.

Rico went to the front porch, sat on the top step, and looked up at the moon. Then he heard a shuffling sound behind him. He looked around and saw Jose standing there.

For a while they said nothing. The night smelled sweet.

"Hey, Rico . . .," Jose said.

"Yeah?"

"Rico . . . when I go back to live in our house again, you and me . . . we can hang out, huh?"

Rico could hardly believe his ears. What Papa said was true, he thought to himself. It was some kind of miracle. It was as if all the badness and anger in Jose had burned up in the fire. Papa said Jose was like the bird called a phoenix, which burned up and then was reborn from its ashes. Sometimes people just need a little help from others, Papa said, to see the goodness in themselves.

"We'll be friends, won't we?" Jose said a little louder.

Rico waited a moment before speaking. "Maybe when you go back home you'll want to beat me up again," he finally said.

"Hey!" Jose sounded as if he'd been wounded. "Don't even joke about that. We're blood brothers now. We stick together no matter what."

"Well," Rico said with a smile, "I guess that means we'll be friends."

Jose's smile beamed back at him. Then Jose spoke quietly, almost to himself. "All right!"

Star  ters

Here are some tips for building self-confidence in yourself and others:

★ Look for the very best in yourself and others.

★ Listen to others—it makes them feel important.

★ Tell others what you like and appreciate about them.

★ Stand up for yourself and what you know is right. It always pays off in higher self-confidence and respect from others.

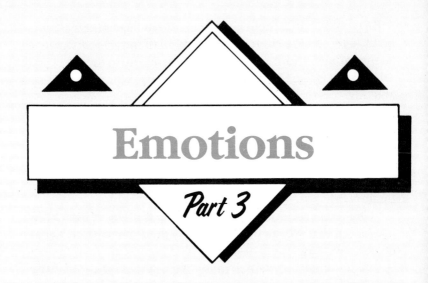

Emotions

Part 3

"There are a lot of feelings I don't share with people. They're the ones that I'm mostly afraid of."

"I can talk to my grandparents about my feelings because I know they'll listen and understand."

"I keep going through these periods when I'm deeply depressed. I try to explain my feelings to others around me, but I can never figure out what's wrong. I keep telling myself it's only a stage I'm going through, but that doesn't really work."

"Sometimes I feel a lot of envy of other people who have things I want. I don't like that feeling, and I really want to get a handle on it. I think that we all should be happy with what we have and be thankful that we have it."

"I can tell my feelings to one of my friends at school, and she really understands. But if I want advice, I go to my mom. Other times I talk to the next-door neighbor's cat. It rubs up against my legs as if it's telling me it understands."

51

"I can tell things to a friend of mine that I've known since childhood. I trust her completely. We tell each other everything."

Feelings! Sometimes it seems as if you're hit by different kinds of feelings all day long. It can be both exciting and confusing. One of the main ideas in this section is that this jumble of feelings is normal for people your age. Another main idea is that you can learn how to get a handle on your feelings—you can understand yourself and be in control.

In his article titled "Understanding and Handling Your Feelings," Gary R. Collins remembers the many different feelings he experienced as an adolescent. Today Gary Collins is a psychologist who works with young people and their families. He understands young people, and he's helped them to work out their problems. Also, he's willing to admit that he had a lot of the same problems himself when he was your age.

The short story for this section, "Caught In the Middle," tells about a 12-year-old boy who has so many confused and unhappy feelings that he'd rather not even think about them. We see in the story that trying to ignore your feelings doesn't work. Your feelings are a part of you. To be happy and healthy, you need to accept and communicate your feelings in positive ways. That way, feelings can be one of the best parts of being alive.

Understanding and Handling Your Feelings

by
Gary R. Collins

ould you describe yourself in just a few words?

When I was your age, I would have picked three words to describe myself: "stupid," "ugly," and "odd."

I thought I was stupid because it always seemed that the teacher asked me questions I couldn't answer. I used to wonder why everybody else in the class got the easy questions and "dumb old Gary" (that was me) got the hard ones. It wasn't long before I started to feel like a real klutz.

Maybe life would have been easier if I had been handsome, athletic, and well built, but I was overweight. I thought I was fat. I would try to slouch in my seat and hide from the teacher, but that was impossible because the girl who sat in front of me was skinny. Sometimes the other kids made comments about my size, and that didn't make me feel any better about myself. My mother thought I was beautiful. But what do mothers know about things like that? I thought I was ugly.

I also felt that I was odd. As far as I knew, I was the only kid my age in the whole world who felt frustrated, criticized by others, and not smart enough to do much of anything, including answering questions.

What I didn't know then was that almost everybody feels stupid at times. Most of us—one expert says 95 percent of us—see things in ourselves that we don't like. Because of that we get especially hurt inside when friends or brothers and sisters tease us and call us names. Even when people say nothing, it's easy to be discouraged because of the braces on your teeth, the zits that won't go away, or the fact that you seem to be a different size from everybody else in the whole school.

Feeling stupid, ugly, and odd is pretty common to young teenagers. It's also common—and normal—sometimes to feel angry, disappointed, rejected, sad, lonely, and guilty. And, as if that weren't enough, young teenagers often go through sudden and unexpected mood changes. You may feel happy one minute and sad the next, hardly even knowing why.

It's Okay to Have Feelings

When I was little we were told that "big boys don't cry" and that nobody likes a "crybaby." Maybe you've heard this too. Sometimes it seems that people think it's bad to express any kind of feelings, even happy ones.

After being warned for long enough not to express our feelings, most of us decide that there must be something wrong with having feelings.

Let's begin, then, by reminding ourselves that everybody has emotions. It's impossible to be human and not have them. Because of feelings, our lives have variety and interest. If we didn't have feelings we would be like robots. We'd be blah, boring, mechanical, and not even able to understand what it means to have fun.

Emotions tend to seem especially intense when you're young. As you get older, the whole range of your feelings becomes more familiar. When you're young, though, it's easy to feel helpless and overwhelmed by emotions. When you start facing your feelings for the first time, things hit with greater force.

Let's suppose, for example, that you and your closest friend are going to be separated because of a family move. Your parents might say "You'll get over it." You probably will, but for a while it may seem that the loneliness and sadness will never go away.

Because your feelings are so strong, your reactions might be strong as well. Little irritations that might not bother an adult or even a younger child can plunge you now into depression and worry. On the brighter side, adolescents have been known to do really crazy things to show their joy and happiness over something like a football victory that maybe isn't all that important. (This isn't a lot different from some adults who get really mad or who jump up and down and shout in excitement over a game on TV. But kids tend to do that kind of thing more freely and more often.)

You and I may not always like our feelings. Our emotions may make life miserable at times. Still, we need to admit that emotions are part of being human. If you try to deny your feelings, you're only kidding yourself.

Emotions Affect Our Bodies

Sometimes people call each other "scaredy-cat," but have you ever thought about why this is such an appropriate expression? Next time you see a scared cat, think about it. When a cat is frightened, its little heart starts beating faster, its muscles get tense, and there are changes in the chemicals in its bloodstream. Although the cat doesn't realize this, its body is getting ready for action. If the danger continues, the animal will do one of two things. It will either do whatever it takes to defend itself, or it will run away as fast as it can.

In many ways something like this also happens to people. When we are excited, angry, scared, or aroused by other emotions, our bodies go through many physical changes. Our hearts beat faster, for example, and our muscles get tense. All of these changes make us more alert and ready to react. We too can defend ourselves or run.

Human beings, however, have a problem that animals never face. If we give way to our feelings and let them take over, we can get into trouble. Have you ever said something in anger— or hit somebody—and regretted it later? Have you ever yelled at a teacher, told somebody that you were lonely, or said you were in love, and then wished later that you had kept your mouth shut? It isn't always wise to express your feelings freely.

Does this mean that it's smarter always to hide our feelings? No! If you keep feelings of anger, frustration, sadness, and bitterness hidden away or bottled up inside, your body stays tense, physical illness can develop, and you can feel churned up inside. It can actually be bad for your health. (It isn't good to keep pleasant feelings inside either; all feelings need to be expressed.)

Feelings that you keep all bottled up inside don't just go away. It's as if you bought a bunch of bananas and stuck them away in a cupboard. You might not be able to see them, but before long you'd smell them. And if you opened the cupboard, chances are you'd see little fruit flies hovering all over them like miniature helicopters. They'd be rotten.

You can try to treat emotions like bananas. You can hide them so they can't be seen and you can pretend they don't exist, but they'll still be around. And, just like those bananas, eventually you'll have to deal with them.

So What Do We Do with Feelings?

Sometimes feelings can make life more exciting; they can also make us miserable. Whenever feelings come along, then, we have to decide whether to "let them out or hold them in"— and to what degree.

Sometimes that decision can be easy. If your team is winning, you have no hesitation about shouting wildly. What do you do, however, if the team is losing and you feel like crying? How do you act when you're really angry at a friend, a teacher, a parent, or your brother? How do you act when the person who makes you most angry is yourself? What do you do when you're feeling disappointed, excited, lonely, or guilty?

The answers to these questions depend on two main things.

First, where are you? Sometimes I cry if I'm really sad, but usually that only happens when I'm alone or with someone who accepts me and doesn't laugh. Crying at a funeral is appropriate. Crying in an ice cream store because they're all out of chocolate chip is not appropriate, unless you happen to be three years old. If you're at a football game, it's okay if you shout or give in to your desire to laugh like a hyena. But you'll get a little static if you do this while you're listening to a sermon in church.

Not long ago I was in South America, where everybody hugs everybody else. It's a normal thing to do in that culture. Try hugging everybody at your junior high school in North America, however, and the other kids are likely to think you're more than a little odd.

How you show your feelings, therefore, depends on where you are.

How you show your feelings also depends on the kind of person you are.

Some people are just a lot more expressive than others. Some are shy, and others like to play it cool and be self-controlled, at least in front of their friends. How, when, and where you express your emotions is a personal thing. A lot depends on your background, your family's way of expressing feelings, and what makes you feel comfortable. It's certain that everybody has feelings, but we express them in different ways.

How To Handle Your Feelings

Can feelings be controlled? This is an important practical question—and the answer is yes. Feelings can be handled.

I remember one time when I was part of my junior high school choir. We must have been pretty good, because our choir was invited to sing in a big concert hall. We were competing with choirs from other schools for some sort of prize.

Everybody was nervous; nobody wanted to make a mistake. When our turn came to sing, we filed up to the platform, stood up straight, and waited for the choir leader's signal to start singing. Everybody began at the same time.

Except me.

I made a mistake and started about two seconds before everybody else. I really felt dumb, singing the first word all by myself, in front of several thousand people, and before the rest of the choir got around to starting. I can laugh about it now, but at the time I was really embarrassed and decided that we had lost the contest because of me. I kept thinking about it for weeks afterwards, and I had the feeling that everybody else in the choir remembered it just as vividly as I did. Maybe you've felt the same kind of embarrassment when you missed an important basketball shot or forgot your lines in the school play.

Feelings are like that. They often stay around and bother us for a long time. They drag us down and even affect the way we think. The first step in handling emotions is to admit your feelings. If you're mad, sad, glad, or having some other kind of feeling, admit it—at least to yourself.

Then think before you act. Do you remember the old idea that when you get mad you should count to ten before exploding? That isn't a bad suggestion. Sometimes a few seconds is all the time you need to stop yourself from saying something harmful or from doing something that you could be sorry for later.

Of course, it isn't always easy to control your feelings and actions. Have you ever had a test in school that worried you or perhaps a big game that you didn't want to lose? Maybe you were really anxious about what was going to happen, and then along came somebody who wanted to help. "It's okay," your friend may have said. "You don't have to worry about this."

Would that stop you from worrying? Absolutely not. Feelings don't go away just because you or somebody else decides that they should.

The best way to deal with feelings is to think about what caused them in the first place. Then we can try to do something about the causes. This leads me to another suggestion that may seem a little strange, but it works: talk to yourself about your feelings.

Some people have suggested that we humans talk to ourselves all the time. Usually we don't do it out loud—that's because we don't want to look crazy and because we don't want others to know what we're telling ourselves. When I was your age, I used to talk to myself about my lack of ability in sports. I have to confess that I'm a terrible athlete. That always made me feel inferior. A lot of kids in my school thought that people who couldn't run fast or hit a baseball probably weren't worth much. At the time I pretty much talked myself into believing that this was true. Now I know that some people are good in athletics and some, like me, are better at other things. I guess I had to talk myself into believing that too.

Not long ago I was watching a track meet with people who could run really fast. When the starting gun sounded, one guy took off like a bullet and soon was ahead of everybody else in the race. The kids from his school cheered like crazy. He was a certain winner, even before the race was half over.

Then he tripped.

For some reason he lost his balance and fell flat on his face in the middle of the track. By the time he got to his feet and ran the rest of the distance, everybody else had crossed the finish line. It wasn't hard to see that this guy was disappointed, disgusted with himself, and fighting mad.

I don't know how he handled his feelings after the race. He could have spent the next few hours—or months—condemning himself, criticizing the "stupid track," and generally making himself and everybody else miserable.

Feelings are like that. Sometimes they take over our minds. But that doesn't have to happen. The runner could have asked himself several key questions. So could you in a similar situation:

- **Why do I feel the way I do?** (Because I made a mistake that caused me to fall in front of all those people, embarrassing me and letting down my school.)

- **What can I do about it now?** (Probably nothing, although it might help to talk to the track coach. He might have some suggestions to keep me from making the same mistake again.)

- **Does my mistake mean that I'm stupid and doomed to be a failure forever?** (Of course not—everybody makes mistakes.)

It's important to be honest with yourself in answering questions like these. Otherwise, the only person you're fooling is the most important person as far as your feelings are concerned —yourself.

Some Other Tips on Handling Feelings

Once you realize the importance of learning how to handle your feelings, you'll start to get into the habit. Next time you're struggling with some emotion, ask yourself the following two questions and try to come up with honest answers:

1. What is causing this feeling?

2. What can I do about it?

If you don't have any good answers, talk with a friend, parent, youth leader, counselor, coach, or teacher. When we're honest enough to share our feelings with another person, we've made an important step in handling how we feel. The sooner you learn this, the easier it will be to deal with your feelings.

Another important idea is to express your emotions without losing your cool. How do you do that? Tell others how you feel—honestly, but without ranting, raving, and making a fool of yourself. Sometimes it helps to use "I Feel" statements. These are sentences that follow the pattern "When something happens...I feel...because...." They let others know your feelings clearly and directly. Here are some examples:

- "When you do things like that, I feel really burned up, because I asked you not to."

- "When you don't listen to me and walk away, I feel hurt because I need you to listen."

- "When I did that, I felt really sorry because I didn't mean to hurt your feelings."

That last one leads me to another suggestion: when you forget all of this fine advice and blow your top, be quick to apologize. I'm a psychologist. People come to me to talk about their problems. So I'd like to be able to tell you that I always handle my emotions beautifully, that I never get discouraged, that I never yell at my kids, and that I'm a model of self-control. Well, don't believe it. Nobody can be perfect, and I'm no exception. At times all of us get carried away by our feelings, including me. The important thing is to be able to admit our mistakes and say we're sorry.

There's another thing you can do: don't let your mind make matters worse. Before I started to write this chapter, I called one of my young friends and we went out for a soft drink. I knew he'd been having some problems. Between sips, my friend told me how he'd felt recently when he was rejected by some of the kids in his youth group. "We were pretty good friends for a while," he said, "but then they kind of cooled off to me. Then they started ignoring me. I guess they decided I wasn't good enough for their group."

Did my friend sit around moping, thinking how awful he was, and planning how he could get revenge? No, he didn't. He admitted to himself that he felt hurt and sad because of what the other kids had done. Then he talked it over with the group leader and made up his mind that he was going to do two things. He would continue to be friendly to the people who were rejecting him. But he'd also get involved in other activities where he could find new friends. He didn't spend time brooding over his feelings so that matters got worse.

This brings us to one last suggestion for handling feelings: be willing to reach out to somebody else. Is there someone you know who is sad, discouraged, lonely, or feeling rejected? By taking a couple of minutes to encourage such people, you can really be a great help to them. What may surprise you is that this can make you feel pretty good as well. Some day you might find that another person will reach out to help you when you feel down.

Everybody has feelings. Emotions are an important part of being human. The more we recognize this—and understand our own and other people's feelings—the better off life will be for everybody.

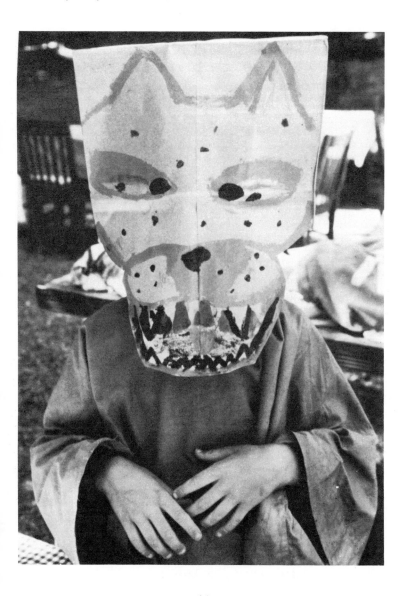

Caught in the Middle

a short story by
Hank Resnik

The car pulled up in front of the house. "Have a good week," Peter's father said. "I'll see you next weekend."

"Thanks for the lift, Dad," Peter said as he opened the car door and threw his bag and tennis racket onto the ground.

"Peter! I just had your racket restrung! Treat it with a little respect."

"It's okay," Peter said. "They're built to take it." He was 12 and growing so fast that his pants were always too short. Most of the time he wore Army clothes and dreamed about flying a computerized helicopter or spaceship like ones he'd seen on television. Army guys don't have to treat things like tennis rackets with respect, he thought to himself. Helicopters, yes, but not tennis rackets.

"See ya, Dad," Peter said. He started to get out of the car but stopped when he felt his father's hand on his arm.

"How about a hug?" his father asked quietly.

Peter had a rush of warm feelings and threw his arms around his father's neck. Then he jumped out of the car and started walking toward the house. "'Bye, Dad," he called without turning to look back.

The house was warm, and Peter could smell dinner cooking. He stopped inside the door and sniffed. He could hardly believe it, but he was sure that his mom had made his two favorite things, barbecued chicken and butterscotch brownies. Something must be happening, Peter thought to himself. He tried not to seem too excited as he walked toward the kitchen.

"Hiya!" his mother said as soon as she saw him, a huge smile on her face. "I think you grew during the week. Oh, it's so good to see you." Peter hugged her as she held him close. Suddenly he realized how much he'd missed her. It was often that way when he went to his father's house, and this time he'd been with his father for a whole week. She swept his brown hair back and forth several times. "You get more handsome all the time," she said.

"Not if I look like a gorilla when you're done messing my hair," he said. They both laughed, and then she hugged him again.

"I missed you so much," his mother said. "It was so strange being away from you all week. How did everything go?"

"Fine. How was everything with you?"

"Everything went all right, huh?"

"Yeah, sure." She never said things twice or sounded dumb. For the first time since he'd come into the house he thought

that maybe something was wrong. "You made my special chicken," he said. "And you made butterscotch brownies. What's the big occasion? Are we celebrating something?"

Peter's mother took a deep breath. "There doesn't have to be any special occasion," she said. "I'm just so happy to be home and see you again. I've never been away from you like this for a whole week."

"Didn't you have a good time with Arthur?" Arthur was his mom's new boyfriend—or whatever people their age called it. Actually Arthur wasn't such a bad guy. But he wished she would say she'd had a terrible time on her visit to see Arthur, who lived all the way across the country (she'd met him during the summer while he was visiting here).

"It was wonderful," she said, that huge smile on her face again.

"So what's wrong?"

"Did I say something was wrong?"

"No, but what's wrong?"

Suddenly his mother had that "Let's get it over with" expression on her face. "Come," she said. "Sit down." Her arm on his shoulder, she guided him over to the kitchen table. They sat there for a while, as if they were waiting to see who would make the first move.

"Peter, Arthur and I are going to be married."

Peter was prepared for the worst, and he showed no reaction at all. "Congratulations," he said.

"Thank you." His mother looked at the table for a moment, then back up at him. "I'm really very happy, and I hope you will be too. Peter, this is what I've been waiting for. I love Arthur very much. And I'll always love you too. Always."

"I'm very happy for both of you," Peter said, again not showing any emotion. "Very." But he noticed his hands were shaking slightly, and there was a sting in his eyes as if he might cry.

Then she was all bouncy again. "Come on. Time for dinner."

During dinner they talked mainly about what was going on at his father's house—the remodeling of the den, how his stepsisters were doing with fractions, whether he was doing any

67

better with fractions, and a variety of other subjects that didn't have much to do with what was really on their minds.

Finally, over the brownies, Peter decided that he had to say something. He couldn't just pretend that one of the most important things in his life wasn't about to happen. "When are you and Arthur going to be married?" he asked.

"In July. I wanted to wait until school was over."

"Why?" Suddenly Peter had a terrible feeling in his stomach. It was almost as if he'd never eaten the wonderful meal at all. He felt sick or hungry or something. He didn't know what he felt.

"Well. . . ." His mother looked at the table for a long time without saying anything. "Arthur has his job he can't leave. He can't move here. So this summer I'll be moving to where he lives." Finally she looked him straight in the eye. "I'll be selling this house and moving."

Peter tried to be cool. When you're in the Army and you land on a beach, he was thinking, if you don't stay cool, you're dead. You have to stay cool. Nevertheless, his body trembled a little. "What about me?" he asked.

"Well, naturally, Arthur wants you to live with us. You haven't met his kids, but you'll love them—two boys and a girl. . . ."

"I know. Two boys and a girl, 18, 17, and 15, and the boys are great at tennis and basketball. You told me." When his mother first told him about the two boys who were so good at tennis and basketball, she probably meant it to sound like some kind of big attraction. All he could think of, though, was that now he would have to be a great athlete too. It would be like some kind of contest to see which one was the neatest kid.

"I know you're going to like them, Peter. And they'll love you. And Arthur loves you."

Somehow he had known all week this would happen. He had been dreading it. All week he'd been hoping that maybe while she was visiting Arthur they'd break up or something. Why did this have to happen? he was thinking to himself. Why did it have to happen to him! It wasn't fair! He clenched his teeth hard and tried to push away all the confusing feelings. "What about Dad?" he finally said.

"I don't know, honey," she said. "We're going to have to work that out. Probably you'll spend summers or vacations with him. I'm not sure how we'll arrange it. But we'll work it out somehow. It's going to be all right—I promise. You'll get to see both of us almost as much as before—it'll just be a different arrangement."

Peter pulled himself to his feet. "I want to lie down for a while," he said. "I'm not feeling too good. Must've eaten too much chicken or something."

His mother didn't try to stop him.

A few days after his mother's return from her visit to Arthur, Peter was sitting in a waiting room reading an old copy of *National Geographic* with an article about space probes that he'd read before. He would rather not be here at all, he was thinking. Probably because his mother knew that, she'd picked him up at school and brought him here. So there was no way out of it. He'd have to talk with the shrink.

This wasn't the first time he'd visited a psychiatrist. The whole family had seen one for a while during and after his parents' divorce. His mother had explained that this woman wasn't really a psychiatrist at all. Her name was just plain "Ellen," his mother said—not "Doctor" anything. She was a person who helped families solve difficult problems. So what? Peter thought to himself. She was a shrink, no matter what you called her. And he didn't like the idea of strangers asking him questions about his secret thoughts.

A door opened on the other side of the waiting room, and a small, gray-haired woman appeared. She wore glasses and her face was full of lines, but her smile was warm and friendly. "Peter?" she asked, looking at him. For a small person, her voice was surprisingly loud and strong. Just from looking at her he

had a feeling that it would be difficult to put anything over on her.

"That's me," he said, standing up. "Time to face the music."

"Come this way," the woman said. "I'm Ellen." She led him into a bright room with a thick blue carpet and several comfortable-looking upholstered chairs. He sat in one of the chairs and found, to his delight, that it bounced slightly. He started bouncing.

"Why do you think coming here means you have to face the music?" Ellen asked, sitting down in one of the larger, more important-looking chairs.

"You don't see a shrink unless there's trouble," Peter replied.

"Do you know why your parents thought it would be a good idea for you to talk with me?"

"It has something to do with my mom getting married again," he said.

Ellen crossed her legs and leaned toward him. She definitely wasn't what you'd call pretty, Peter was thinking, but he liked her anyway. She really seemed to want to talk with him. "You and your parents need to make some difficult decisions," she said.

"Yeah."

"It's a very happy time for your mother because she's going to marry someone she loves, but in some ways it's an unhappy time for all of you too."

"You can say that again!" Looking around the room, Peter noticed a big wooden box in a corner. "Is that box full of toys?" he asked.

"Why?"

"I just wondered. When was a little kid, my parents took me to a psychiatrist because I was having problems in school, and the psychiatrist had a big box like that filled with toys."

"As a matter of fact, there are some toys in there," Ellen said. "But I think we need to talk about you and your parents. This is a difficult situation you're all in together."

"I know," Peter said. "They're fighting a lot. Sometimes he comes over and they spend hours arguing. Just like the old days."

"I'm trying to help them work out some of their problems," Ellen said.

"Yeah, like what to do with me."

It seemed as if a great deal of time went by before Ellen spoke again. "What would you like to happen?"

"I think the whole thing stinks!" Peter said, his voice suddenly very loud. "I don't care what happens."

Ellen's voice was quiet. "It doesn't sound as if you don't care."

"I'm mad at both of them," Peter said. "They should never have gotten divorced. They should never have gotten married!"

"Peter," Ellen said, "I know that you're upset about this, but the problem isn't going to go away. Your mother and father and I need to know how you're feeling and what you want. We need to know where you want to be. I realize it's very difficult and even painful for you, but I'll never repeat anything you say here. I need to know what you want."

"This is a trap," Peter said. "You just got me in here to make me choose." He stood up and looked down at her. "Well, I won't choose. You can't make me choose. You can torture me and I still won't choose." He was crying now, even as he shouted at her. The tears came streaming down his face. He'd wanted to cry for a long time. He felt angry and sad and confused all at once.

Ellen's voice was very quiet. "Sit down, Peter. No one is going to make you choose between your parents. I just wanted to know how you feel. . . ."

Peter sat down again and hid his head in his arms. "I'm not talking," he said. "Sorry. You seem like a nice lady, but I'm not talking. Maybe you should give my parents their money back. I don't care what you say. I am not talking."

Peter was true to his word. Ellen kept asking him questions, but 40 minutes later the session was over, and he left the office without answering a single one of them.

After school several weeks later, Peter was huddled in the big old dirty armchair in the family room watching a soap opera, when the phone rang. He put the receiver to his ear and heard a screaming, siren-like sound. It was so loud that it almost hurt. Then it stopped. Then a voice said, "This is Captain Johnson. The navigator has just sighted an unknown planet. It could be a Death Star, but it could also be a new planet where . . . ."

Peter interrupted, saying, "Terry! Give me a break! Can't you just say 'hello'!"

"Aw, c'mon," said the voice on the phone in its more normal Peter's-best-friend-Terry tone. "This is probably the closest I'll ever come to being a captain of a spaceship. Let me enjoy it."

"Go ahead and enjoy it," Peter said. "Just don't make me get a headache."

"So what are you doing?" Terry said. "You busy this afternoon?"

"Am I busy!" Peter said. "This is the afternoon that I go with my parents to face the music."

"Oh," Terry said. "Too bad. I was gonna ask if you wanted to meet me over at the park."

"Nah, I can't."

"Too bad. Well, I gotta go."

"I'll see you in school tomorrow," Peter said.

"Yeah. By the way, I didn't really see a new planet. I made up that part. But the spaceship is real."

"Yeah. Real funny." Peter hung up the phone without another word. But he knew it was okay. One thing about a best friend was that you could hang up the phone on him and he'd still be your best friend. Of course, if he had to live with his mom and Arthur, he'd probably never see Terry again. But if he lived with his dad, he'd always be missing his mom.

A new soap opera was just about to begin when Peter heard his mother's key in the front door. "Peter!" she called out. Then she came into the room. "Peter, are you ready to go? We have to be there in a few minutes."

"Ready when you are," Peter said.

"Well, you don't look ready. The least you could have done was brush your hair. Come on! Turn off the TV. We have to

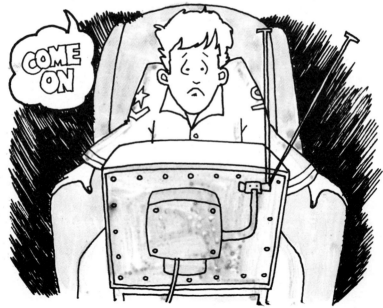

hurry. And brush that hair!'' He knew the whole afternoon was going to be a disaster. She hardly ever talked to him in such an angry voice.

In the car neither of them spoke much. Mainly, his mother muttered about the traffic and complained about all the hours she was missing from her job at the library because of the appointment. Peter decided that the best thing to do was keep his mouth shut.

His father had arrived before them. He was seated in one of the plastic-cushioned chairs in the waiting room, staring at nothing. Peter couldn't decide which one of his parents looked worse. ''Hi, Dad,'' he said.

His father just looked up at him and smiled, almost as if he wasn't quite sure who Peter was. ''Hi, son'' he said. ''How're you doing?''

''I'm okay,'' Peter said. Then he sat in one of the plastic-cushioned chairs himself.

They waited in silence. Peter realized he had that same sick and empty feeling in his stomach that he'd been feeling a lot lately. ''Time to face the music,'' he said to no one in particular. He looked at his mother and then his father. Both of them just smiled weakly but didn't say anything. Then Ellen appeared in the doorway.

''Hello,'' she said cheerfully. ''Come on in.'' They filed silently into Ellen's office and seated themselves in the comfortable chairs.

''You all understand why you're here,'' Ellen began. ''You've asked me to help you make a very difficult decision about where Peter is going to live after his mother's marriage. This has been a difficult and painful time. I've talked with all of you—well, not very much really with Peter. But, Peter, I've talked with both your parents many, many times. And I can assure you that all they want is the best thing for you. Everyone would be a lot happier if there weren't any decisions to make. But there are. I want to tell you now what my recommendation is. And then I want to take some time for all of us to say how we feel about it. Is there anything anyone wants to say?''

74

For a long time no one spoke. In the silence that opened up among them, Peter's thoughts began to wander. It was as if he weren't here in this room at all. He could almost feel his mind floating away from his body. Maybe, he thought to himself, someday he'd invent a machine that would make people disappear. You'd just press a button and you'd go flying up into the air, so you could get away from people you didn't want to talk with or places where you didn't want to be or feelings you couldn't bear. What a great idea! he thought. All you'd have to do would be to press this magic button . . . .

Star  ters

Ever feel like you're on an emotional roller coaster? One day you're feeling happy—the next day you're feeling sad. Adolescence is a time of changing feelings, sometimes from one hour to the next. So hold on to the handlebars, enjoy the ride and remember:

★ Feelings are an important part of being human—of being you.

★ It's normal and healthy to have a wide range of feelings during this time of life. Accept them.

★ Feelings are triggered by different situations, and everyone has different reactions. This is what makes people unique.

★ It's important to respect other people's feelings. They're as real as your feelings.

★ When you learn to understand and express you feelings, you'll have control over them. They won't control you.

Friends

Part 4

"It's difficult to have more than one best friend because the other one gets jealous."

"I think my friends like the way I'm outgoing and not too many things bother me. I also think they like the way I listen and give advice. And they know they can trust me."

"The most important thing to me about my friends is knowing that they're always there when I need them."

"Friends are very important to me. I think that friends are people you can be weak with. They let you be yourself. They let you make mistakes and be a fool. They forgive you."

"I never expected to get into an argument with my best friend that lasted for more than a week, but it happened recently. We've been friends for ten years."

"One time my friend and I went to our old school and sat on the monkey bars and talked for an hour and a half. It felt great!"

When you're entering adolescence, having friends may be the most important thing in life. As we see in this section, though, some kids will do almost anything to have friends. The section focuses on some key questions: Do you know how to be a good friend? What are you willing to do to make friends? Will you go against what you believe is right? The section helps to guide you in finding some answers for yourself.

Barbara Varenhorst, the author of the article titled "Deciding to Be the Friend You Want," has written a whole book for teenagers about friendship. She's also the founder of a program that teaches students how to be peer counselors. As we see in her article, she understands how difficult it can be sometimes to make choices when peer pressure is involved.

The short story, "Between Friends," focuses on changes in friendships. It tells about two 13-year-olds who are about to go off on very different life paths. Through the story we see that "growing apart" can be a sad time in a friendship—but it's also part of growing up.

Deciding to Be the Friend You Want

by
Barbara Varenhorst

"What are you going to be when you grow up, Charlie Brown?"
"Lonesome."

Charlie's answer may make you laugh—a little. But now that you're starting to be a grown-up yourself, you may not think it's so funny. You're becoming an adolescent; things have changed and are changing all the time. Maybe sometimes you feel lonesome—or afraid and confused. Maybe you're concerned about having friends and being popular.

The pain, confusion, and loneliness are real. Sometimes other people don't believe or understand that. For example, your mom or dad may brush off your feelings and tell you not to worry. Perhaps they've forgotten how much they needed friendships and acceptance when they were your age. The feeling of not being understood just adds to the feeling of loneliness.

Yet you do need friends. Your peers are a vital part of your life.

79

This is normal. Every one of your classmates has similar feelings and thoughts, even though it may not seem that way. That's why everyone your age needs help learning how to become the kind of friend that people want and need.

The Choices You'll Have to Make

The problems you might face in friendships fall into three large "baskets." Each basket contains the major choices you will have to make that affect who you are, the kinds of friends you will have, and what you will do with your life. One basket is labeled "Peer Pressure Decisions"; another, "Hide or Declare Yourself Decisions"; and the third, "Giving and Receiving Decisions." I'm going to describe each basket and suggest ways to cope with each kind of decision.

Peer Pressure Decisions

One of the most important things to think about in dealing with peer pressure decisions is who you really are and what you really want. But sometimes that isn't so easy. Each of us carries around two "selves." One is our outer self—how we look, what we wear, and what we say or do. The other self is the inner self that few people know or see.

Because we want people to like and admire us, many of us work hard to change our outer selves so we'll get the right label—"cool," "popular," or whatever. We try to say the right things, wear certain clothes, and even pretend to know things to impress others. Some people call this playing a role or being phony.

Some say it's just not being yourself. The inner person that people can't see is the "who you really are." It is the self that doesn't change every time you change your appearance. The more you are "true" to your inner self, the more alike your inner and outer selves will be.

Who Decides for You? You or Your Friends?

If you're like most people your age, you're often uncertain about who you really want to be and whether you're good enough (in other words, who you really are). You may have a great fear of being mocked—of being considered weird or different. What if your classmates laugh, put you down, or shut you out of the group? Sometimes you feel you'd be willing to do anything to keep that from happening. When your fear is this great, you may be so eager to be liked by your peers that you're willing to let them decide things for you. That is called "peer pressure."

Because peer pressure is a powerful "decider" in everyone's life, let's examine just how it works. If we understand the different ways it affects us, we may know how to resist it better when we want to.

Suppose the most popular boy in the class asks to borrow your notes to study for an important test tomorrow, but you'd planned on using the notes yourself. What will you do? What if your best friend wants you to join him or her in stealing some tapes from the local record store? Would you do it to keep the friendship or to be accepted? What about times when you may have joined in making fun of someone or said mean things about your parents just because everyone else was doing it? Do you think other kids liked you more because you did these things?

Your peers may pressure you to do something you don't want to do, but at other times you may be absolutely sure it's what you want to do. Suppose your parents have forbidden you to go to a certain movie that "everyone" has seen. A group of your friends is going to see it this Saturday afternoon. You're dying to go too. You tell your friends you can't go, but they say you'll miss the best movie of the year, just because of your pushy parents. So you lie to your parents and tell them you have a baby-sitting job. And suppose that while you're with your friends on Saturday afternoon, the mother for whom you said you were baby-sitting calls and wants to talk to you. Your lie is discovered. Besides being punished, you realize you've lost your parents' trust. They may now question your honesty in all situations. That's quite a price to pay for a movie.

At such times it may help to ask yourself why your "friends" would try to get you to do something that you don't want to do or that you know you shouldn't do. Why would friends try to get you to lie to your parents, be unkind to others, or experiment with drugs? It's possible that they're trying to make themselves feel more grown-up or important or "cool." To feel this, they need you and others to go along with them.

One of the basic laws of human life is that things are to be used and people are to be loved. When friends want you to do something that might hurt you or get you into trouble to serve their own needs, they are using you. But people can't use you unless you let them. Here is the basic question: Are you going to let others use you, or are you going to decide for yourself?

Some Tips on How to Decide for Yourself

In making the decision about whether or not to go along with peer pressure, to consider the consequences of each of your choices.

Here are two possible consequences to think about. First, giving in to peer pressure may actually lose the respect of those you hope to impress. No one really values someone who can be used, manipulated, or pressured. For a while they may fake friendship and respect, but, in the end, others may feel they can toss you aside when you are no longer useful to them.

Another consequence might be the opposite. What if you said to your friends, "No, I can't go with you to the movie on Saturday. My parents have said I can't, and I don't want to go against their wishes." Even if you think your parents are being too strict, you may find afterwards that you like yourself a little more and feel more in control. You may find also that you have gained some respect in the eyes of your peers.

But it takes strength to refuse to go along with the crowd. Consider how much strength it must have taken in the following true story.

This story takes place in a fairly typical high school. Most of the students spend a lot of their time worrying about what others think. If you are anybody, you belong to a clique, and the clique decides how you dress and what you do and say.

Each morning during break time all the cliques gather around the school's courtyard to watch the other kids and check out what is going on. If you want to get to the other side of the courtyard, you never walk across the courtyard or you might get laughed at.

One rainy morning while this was going on, a not very attractive girl carrying a load of books started across the courtyard. She must have been a new student because she didn't know the "rules." Just about in the middle of the courtyard, she tripped and fell, spread-eagled, her books all over. Immediately the jeering and laughter erupted. Then suddenly a boy started walking out to her. As he got nearer, the laughter began to get quieter. When he got to her, he helped her up and began picking up her books. As the two of them started walking to where she was going, there was utter silence. Then, still in silence the students began to scatter, leaving the scene that had wiped the jeers and name calling from their lips.

This story is a powerful example of how one young person stood up to peer pressure. The boy who helped the girl in such an embarrassing situation must have been a person who felt good about himself. Otherwise, he wouldn't have had the courage to do what he did.

What would you have done if you had been in the crowd that morning? What would your friends have done? Would you like this boy to be your friend?

Can You Learn to Say "No"?

Most of the decisions you make won't be nearly as dramatic as that. They will come up suddenly when you least expect them, giving you little time to think. People who want to make their own decisions and not be pressured by their peers usually know this and are prepared with a plan for handling the situation.

One girl told me that when kids pressure her to smoke dope, she tells them she can't because she's allergic to it. Then they don't hassle her. Even a simple, straightforward, "No, I don't want to" or "Sorry, I can't" can be an effective way of handling peer pressure. If you practice saying this alone in your own room, you may find you have the courage to say it aloud when you need to.

Lisa, a young friend of mine, told me that until she made an important decision for herself, she used to go to her high school parties and drink. She liked the drinking because she felt more social and "with it," but she didn't like the way it made her feel. She began thinking of the consequences. Finally she decided she no longer wanted to drink. But when she went to parties she still found it hard to resist. At that point Lisa decided that if a party was going to have drinking, she wouldn't go. Because of this decision, she missed some of the fun she used to have, but the self-respect she gained was more important.

Once you've decided you want to say "No" to peer pressure, you need practice to develop the skill of taking a stand without coming across as rude, aggressive, of self-righteous. This is what is called being assertive. But to be assertive, you have to believe you have a right to say "No." This doesn't mean you have to be mean or nasty. It does mean that you have a right to demand that others accept your decision.

Will You Lose Your Friends?

Saying "No" to peer pressure takes courage, especially if "everybody's doing it." But sometimes friendships have to be tested. A real friend doesn't say "I'll be your friend if . . . ." Instead, a real friend says "I'll be your friend no matter what."

If you find that you're frequently in conflict with what your group of friends wants to do, maybe you'll decide to find a new group of friends who support you and your values.

Hide or Declare Yourself Decisions

You're at an age when having friends is one of the most important things in life. But real friendship is almost the opposite of going along with peer pressure.

Why is this so? One of the main consequences of giving in to peer pressure is that you may always be faking who you are, and your friendships will also be fake. People are real friends when they can say to each other, "Here I am. Take me or leave me." To say that, or live it, takes courage.

Some of your friends, and perhaps you too, try to escape from peer pressure by wearing "masks" or by building a shell around the inner self for protection. As one boy your age said, "You see, my shell keeps you away. I'm safe in here. I will never be laughed at." Maybe you've never realized that many people who act stuck-up or egotistical are really fearful inside themselves, not really liking who they think they are. Also, people who appear gruff or unkind may actually be tenderhearted and giving under the surface.

Why do you suppose they put on these shells or masks? Often the answer is the one offered by John Powell, the author: "I'm afraid to tell you who I am, because if I tell you who I am, you may not like who I am, and it's all that I have."

How Will You Share Yourself with Others?

Whether to hide or reveal yourself to others in an honest way is another important decision that you will have to make. It won't just happen by itself, and it may require you to learn some new "people" skills. If you decide to declare yourself, you'll be taking the first step toward making real friends. Let me explain what I mean by "declare" and "reveal" yourself to others.

If you were to make a list of the qualities you want in a friend, you would probably include that a friend is someone you can talk with openly and trust. That means a person who is willing to share feelings that are very personal.

We all have feelings that we talk about with almost anyone— like how we feel about a teacher, a movie, or a popular song.

We also have feelings we don't talk about very often—like our fears, our feelings of shame or disappointment, or even sometimes our feelings of pride or joy. And we don't tend to talk about feelings that confuse us or bother us for one reason or another.

Declaring and being open about our innermost feelings is one of the most important elements in a real friendship. It makes the difference between a friendship and just an acquaintance. The reason for this is that the feelings you don't talk about are often the center of who you are. If you don't share them, no one will ever know who you really are!

Of course, there are other things that draw people together besides sharing feelings. Not all our times with friends need to be spent in deep or serious conversation. Doing things together that you enjoy and learning skills or hobbies from one another are an important part of friendship too. A friend is someone who's seen the same movie you've seen and has the same favorite character or scene. A friend is someone with whom you share fun and adventures, and conversations and sometimes just fooling around. Out of these contacts often come the desire and courage to share the special feelings we entrust only to special friends.

It takes courage and practice to be open with one another. Practice will help you learn how to judge whether others are worthy of trust.

People don't always deserve the trust we place in them. But I hope you won't be disillusioned. We learn by trial and error, and this applies to friendship as well. Some people go around sharing personal feelings with anyone, but that's not what I mean by true friendship. A true friend is special. As you explore friendships, you'll learn how to recognize those people who will accept what you share, handle it gently, and treat it as a special gift.

Giving and Receiving Decisions

We all need friends. But too many of us want friends just to satisfy our own needs or to make us feel less lonely. Wanting friends for these reasons isn't bad. But if these are our only reasons for wanting friends, we're using people. Remember, people are to be loved, not used. Real friendship goes beyond getting for oneself. It means giving, caring, and doing for others. One of the ways people make friends is by giving friendship to another without expecting anything in return.

I know this is true after helping hundreds of young people your age to become involved with others through the peer counseling program that I direct. Through this program, I have seen many students find ways to join with others to turn peer pressure into peer support. Here's one true and vivid example:

> Gloria was not an attractive girl; nor was her personality very appealing. Early in peer counseling training she began to talk about her many problems. She had few friends, her home situation was miserable, and she didn't like herself. Even though she was seeing a psychiatrist regularly, she couldn't shake her depression. I became deeply concerned but kept this concern to myself.
>
> As the sessions progressed, I began to sense a difference in Gloria and feel that something was happening. Then, during our last session, I found out why. The other students in the group had also sensed Gloria's needs. So, without my knowledge, they had organized themselves to make daily contact with her, even on the weekends. They would check in with her to see how she was doing or just stop to have a friendly chat. Now, as the class was ending, Gloria told the group what this had meant. She said she couldn't have made it without their friendship. She now felt that there was a reason for living.

These 13-year-olds taught me that people your age can be extremely sensitive to the needs of others. They can learn about the need to reach out to others and some ways of doing it. Do you realize you can do this too? You don't need a peer counseling class to get you started. You do need the desire.

How Can You Be a Good Friend?

"What are you going to be when you grow up, Charlie Brown?" (or any of you who are reading this book?)

"A caring friend who likes myself, who makes decisions for myself, and who is willing to share myself and my feelings with others." Is this your reply? I hope so.

There is a large statue in the African country of Ghana showing a hand holding an egg. The message is that if the hand holds the egg too loosely it will fall out and break. But if the hand holds it too firmly, the egg will be crushed.

We can learn something from this statue about friendships. It takes a certain kind of hand, or person, first to reach out to others and then to cradle, protect, and support the friendships that develop. Decide what kind of hand—or friendship—you would like to support you and how you would like to feel within that friendship. Then become that kind of person yourself. You will have learned a lot about how to be a friend.

"Friendship is born at the moment when one person says to another, 'What, you too? I thought I was the only one.'"

Between Friends

a short story by
Hank Resnik

hilip was in his room doing his homework when the phone rang. He heard his mother answering it in the kitchen. Then her voice came echoing up the stairs: "PHILIP! For you. Don't stay on long—I'm expecting some calls from my church group." Philip padded out to the hall in his stocking feet, plopped down on the carpet, and picked up the receiver of the telephone that lay on the floor.

"What do you say when an elephant goes stampeding through a department store and breaks everything in sight?" said a familiar voice.

Philip thought for a moment and then said, "I give up."

"Tusk, tusk."

"Ooooh!" Philip said. "Bad! Bad, bad, bad!"

"But original," said the voice. "A Nathan Jones original. I don't hear you coming up with any great ones, Mr. Davis."

"You didn't give me a chance," Philip said. "What did one elephant say to another elephant when they met in a small closet?" Silence. "He said, 'Haven't I bumped into you somewhere?'"

"Six on a scale of ten. No more than six."

"Hey, Nathan, get serious. I have two hours of math homework to do."

The response was a kind of gasping sound. Then a sick-sounding voice said, "Math! All I have to do is hear the word and I have trouble breathing. You—Philip Davis—will be

93

responsible for your best friend's death. I can see the headlines now . . . ."

"PHILIP!" Philip's mother's voice came ringing up the stairs like a great bell. "I'm expecting calls. Are you still on?"

"Be off in a sec," Philip called back. Then, into the phone, "I gotta go. My mom's expecting calls."

"Well, I'll see ya 'round, dude. Watch out for stampeding elephants."

"I'll see you too, dude," Philip said. "But I won't be in school tomorrow—remember?"

"You playing hooky or something?"

"Tomorrow, dummy, is the day I take the test to get into Richmond High School. It's my big day, my big chance. Now I gotta go so I can rest my mind after all this heavy thinking."

On the other end of the line there was a long silence. To Philip the silence was so silent it was loud.

"PHILIP!" This time Philip's mother was standing at the bottom of the stairs. "Off the phone this minute!"

"Gotta go, Nate," Philip said into the phone. But he wished

Nathan would say something—anything.

Finally Nathan spoke. "Don't think too hard, Mr. Genius. It might burn out your brain."

Philip hung up the phone. Then he called downstairs to his mother, "I'm off, Mom. Sorry I took so long."

"I just wish I didn't have to say it three times," his mother grumbled.

"But Mom," Philip said in a playful tone. "I'm a teenager. I'm going through my period of rebellion. I'm supposed to be difficult."

"Very funny," his mother said.

"Anyway," Philip continued, "I don't think you need to worry about me and Nathan spending so much time on the phone any more. If I get in to Richmond High, he'll probably never talk to me again."

"That is not very funny," Philip's mother said. "It might even be true. And if it were true, I'd be very, very sorry."

Just then the phone rang. "That's for me, I'm sure," his mother said, rushing off to the kitchen.

Philip was glad. If the conversation had continued, he might have had to admit how upset he was. For weeks now, he and Nathan had been arguing about Philip's decision to take the test for Richmond High. It was the school where students with the best grades went, the ones who would probably go on to the best universities. Nathan said Philip would be selling out if he went to Richmond. For Nathan, school was a kind of game, the object being to avoid as much work as possible. Philip had a completely different attitude.

If the conversation with his mother had continued, Philip might have had to admit that he'd almost rather lose the chance to go to Richmond High than lose his best and oldest friend. But for the moment he kept his thoughts to himself.

The morning of the day after the Richmond High entrance test, Philip was walking down the hall of Franklin Junior High School toward his English honors class. He was so absorbed in his thoughts that he didn't notice his friend Nathan approaching from the other direction. "Hey, blood, slap me ten!" Nathan said.

Philip smiled as he stuck out his hands, palms up. "Hey, blood!" he said. Nathan slapped the palms of his hands with a loud crack. Then he said loudly, "Now the black-hand side, brother." Philip turned his hands over, and Nathan slapped his hands again. It was one of their favorite greetings.

But today there was a strange glint in Nathan's eye. And he'd slapped Philip's hands extra hard—so hard that they actually stung a little.

"Did I tell you I went to a hotel where they had a bed that was twice as long as usual?" he said.

Philip decided to go along with the joking. "That sounds like a lot of bunk to me," he said. "I just heard that one too."

"Well, then, how do you get an elephant to sit down with you at the dinner table?" Nathan asked. It sounded like a challenge.

"Very, very carefully."

"You stole it! I know you did!"

"I did not steal it," Philip said. "It's in the elephant joke book I gave you for your birthday."

"You shouldn't read joke books that you give to people for their birthdays," Nathan said. "It's very rude. Rude 'n' crude."

"Mrs. Benson is going to think I'm very rude if I don't get to English class," Philip said.

Now the look in Nathan's eyes was downright unfriendly. "Oh, you wouldn't dream of being late," Nathan said in a mocking voice. "You wouldn't dream of offending dear Mrs. Benson."

Suddenly Philip was angry too. "Lay off it, Nate. I gotta go."

"Yeah," Nathan said. "You gotta go to fancy English honors class, and you probably gotta go to fancy Richmond High School too."

So that was it! "All I did was take the test," Philip said. "I didn't say I was gonna go. I may not even get in."

"Oh, you'll get in," Nathan said. "And then you'll go. And then you'll turn into this creepy genius. I bet the only thing the kids at Richmond High think about is what universities they're applying to."

The bell rang. "Now I am late for class," Philip said. "Thanks a lot. Thanks for nothing. Some friend you are."

Conversation at the Davis's dinner table usually meant everyone trying to get a word in at once. This was hardly surprising, considering that the Davis family consisted of two parents and six children. Finally, though, everybody stopped talking long enough to pay some serious attention to a chocolate pie that Aretha, Philip's 16-year-old sister, had made as a project for her cooking class.

"Philip," said Philip's father, "I have a feeling something's bothering you. Got a problem?"

"I'd rather not talk about it," Philip said. The rest of the family stared at him. "It's something . . . I don't want to talk about it."

"I bet I know," said Arthur, Philip's older brother. "It's about Nathan." He'd overheard many of Philip and Nathan's telephone conversations, and he also played basketball with them sometimes.

Philip spoke through clenched teeth. "I don't want to talk about it."

Suddenly Philip's father seemed very determined. "Arthur and Aretha, I want you to supervise the cleanup tonight. Philip, I think we need to have a little meeting."

"Definitely," said Philip's mother. "Let's go into the study."

When the three of them were seated in the comfortable chairs of the study, a book-filled room where most high-level meetings of this kind were held, Philip's father was the first to speak. His voice was gentle. "We have to know what's bothering you, son. This is not a family where people keep secrets from each other."

"I don't think there's much you can do," Philip said, looking at the floor.

"Just tell us about it," his mother said in her most understanding voice. "Sometimes when you just talk, things don't seem so bad."

"I've been thinking...," Philip said. Then he stopped himself. His parents waited patiently. "I've been thinking that even if I get in to Richmond High I'm not going to go. I can go to Jones High, where all the other kids are going. Where Nathan's going."

Philip's father looked at Philip's mother as if to say "I told you so!" Then he turned to Philip. "It would be really hard to break out of the mold, wouldn't it?" he said quietly. "But isn't that what you want to do? Do you know what the choice is?"

"Yes!" Philip felt angry and confused. "You've told me a million times. You have to work hard to get a good education, and if you're black you have to run twice as fast as white folks just to keep up with them. I've heard it a million times."

"Do you believe it?" Philip's father asked.

"I don't know," Philip said.

"You don't know, Philip?" his mother said. "After all your years of hard work at school you don't know what you want to do and what your goal is? Tell me, who was saying the other day about how he wanted to go to a good university and become a doctor so he could help other people? Was that you? Or was that someone else?"

Philip glared at his mother without saying anything. Tears had come to his eyes. "I don't want to lose my friends!" he said.

"Yes," his father said. "Your friends are very important. Friends should be important. But tell me, son, what direction is Nathan going in? What is Nathan's goal? Is that your goal?"

"I don't know what my goal is any more!" Philip said. "I can't keep doing things just because it's what you want."

"You're right," his mother said. "Your goals don't mean anything at all unless you really believe in them."

Philip's father nodded in agreement. "If you go to Richmond High School, it won't be for our benefit. I don't want you blaming us if you go there and have to do all that hard work. You'd better be darn sure that you're doing it for yourself."

"So," Philip's mother said, "it looks like you have some big decisions to make. Whatever you do, we believe it'll be what's right. We have a lot of confidence in you, Philip."

"You mean it's up to me?" Philip asked.

"Philip, we could tell you we hope you'll go to Richmond High School and we'd be disappointed if you don't," his father said. "And that would be true. But it has to be something you really want. Otherwise, you're just going through the motions."

"I agree," his mother said. "I agree completely."

The conversation seemed to have ended. Philip was more confused than ever. He'd expected them to be horrified by the idea that he might not go to Richmond High, but here they were, being understanding. "I have homework to do," Philip said finally. "Excuse me."

P hilip lay on his bed for several hours that night, listening to his radio and thinking. Every once in a while he picked

up an old photograph lying on the bed next to him and looked
at it. The photograph showed him and Nathan, arms around
each other's shoulders, grinning hugely for the camera. It had
been taken four years earlier, the first summer they went to Boy
Scout camp together.

Finally Philip got up from the bed, went out to the hallway,
found the telephone at the end of its long cord, took it back into
his room with him, and dialed the number he'd dialed so many
times before. Nathan answered the phone after half a ring.

"I just had a fight with Dracula," Philip said.

"What happened?"

"He really chewed me out."

"Boy's Life, December 1982."

"Shoot! You weren't supposed to remember it."

"I got a brain too, you know. I can even remember things.
I'm smarter than you think."

"You're as smart as anyone I know, stupid."

"Well, thank you for the compliment," Nathan said mockingly.

"You're super smart. You're as smart as I am."

"What is this? You want to borrow money or something?"

"I want you to know that I'm gonna go to Richmond High School—if I get in. And I think I'll get in. I'm gonna go because I have to. It may be the most important thing I ever do in my life. I have to try." Philip waited for an answer. His heart was pounding fast.

"Yeah, I know," Nathan finally said. "It's okay, dude."

"So lay off me, will ya? Stop talking about it the way you do. Okay? 'Cause I'm gonna do it no matter what you say."

Nathan sighed a long, loud sigh that sounded like wind coming through the telephone wire. "I hear ya," he said. "Sure. You gotta do what you gotta do." His voice sounded very sad.

"That's right," Philip said. "I gotta do this. For myself!"

"Well, hey, man," Nathan said. "I better get some sleep. I'll catch ya later."

"Yeah," Philip said. "Catch ya later." Very slowly he hung up the telephone.

For a long time all Philip could do was cry into his pillow. With each sob he felt as if someone were pulling his insides right out of his body. Every time he stopped crying, he opened his eyes to see the picture of himself and Nathan at Scout camp and then cried some more.

The crying was something he had to do before moving on.

One afternoon a few days later, Philip was playing basketball in the schoolyard near his house. He hadn't seen Nathan for several days. Since most of Philip's classes were honors sections, he and Nathan could have gone for months without seeing each other.

The basketball players were the usual crowd—Lonnie, James, Skip, Leroy, William, and several of the others. Philip wondered where Nathan was, but he didn't ask.

101

Sweat dampened Philip's T-shirt as he played. Running and dodging, shooting from all over the court, he was feeling great. After a beautiful jump shot, he was startled to hear loud clapping and a familiar voice saying, "Way to go, dude. Lookin' good!"

Nathan was smiling at him from the sidelines. Really smiling.

"Hey, Nathan!" Philip shouted. "Wanna play?"

"Yeah, sure," Nathan said. Philip looked hard at Nathan. As Nathan jogged on to the court, he reached out his arm, slapped Philip's hand, gave him a big smile, and said, "How you doin'?"

"I'm all right. How you doin'?"

"All right."

Then they played ball.

It wasn't until much later that Philip realized this was the beginning of a new and different kind of friendship.

Star  ters

Here are some "friendly" reminders about friendship:

★ To have friends you have to be a friend.

★ Make time for friends. Friendship means thinking about others, not just yourself.

★ A real friend is honest, open, and willing to take the good times with the bad.

★ A real friend doesn't say "I'll be your friend if . . . ." Real friends won't push you to do something that you know is wrong for you.

Family

Part 5

"I admire the family that can joke, have a good time together, communicate, and love."

"I only talk to my friends because I don't feel my parents understand me. Or they don't want to. They hassle me over decisions, choices, friends, and everything. So I won't talk to them about important things."

"I'm 14 and I'm pretty mature for my age. But whenever I get into trouble I get sent to my room. It's mainly a problem with my mom. Most of the time I think she sends me to my room because she's afraid of all the things that could happen to me. I wish she'd stop running from the fact that I'm growing up. Sending me to my room is not the answer."

"Usually I keep things to myself, but when I do talk it's to my mom and dad. When it's my mom they're usually emotional things. I can talk to them about anything, even stuff that's heavy, like drugs and sex. Not everybody's parents are like that, and, believe me, I know just how lucky I am."

"This may sound weird, but I really like it when I'm alone with my mom, the TV and radio are off, it's completely quiet, and we're in the kitchen. We have to be in the kitchen. I don't know why, but I feel so comfortable just sitting on the counter, late at night, rapping with my mom. You'd have to meet her to understand. She's the most honest, open, loving, sincere person that I know. And even when I'm mean and rotten and evil to her, I know she will always be there."

Families are changing today, but no matter what kind of family you have, it's one of the most important things in making you the person you are. One of the main ideas in this section is the need to appreciate our families—to love and support each other no matter what the family's problems may be. But problems do occur in families, and this section offers ideas about how to deal with them.

Charlie W. Shedd is a family counselor who has helped many different families with almost any problem you can think of. In his article "You and Your Family," he describes the many issues that families are faced with from one day to another—housework, who gets to use the telephone, curfews, and lots of others. The article also offers some basic rules on how to make things better in your family. Follow them, and see how well they can work for you.

The short story, "No Party for Nancy," contrasts two very different kinds of families. Nancy's family is "strict." Her parents want to know where she is and what she's doing most of the time. Claudia's parents let her do just about whatever she wants—they hardly seem to care. Who do you think is better off—Nancy or Claudia? The story answers this question in a way that may surprise you.

You and Your Family

by
Charlie W. Shedd

H ave you ever been in a helicopter? It's a fun ride—slow enough to see things you can't see from a fast plane and low enough to pick up details you might miss from the ground.

This chapter will be a helicopter ride over your family: their emotions, their hurts, and some good things. The chapter will help you to understand your family better, and it may even help them understand you. The chapter describes some basic ideas that have made lots of families happier together.

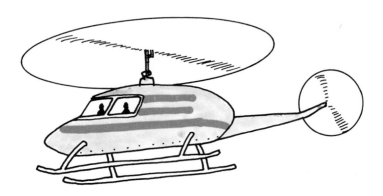

I. The Problems of Family Life

Daddy, You Left the Door Open

Many of the letters I receive are full of complaints. But now and then I get one like this:

> Dear Dr. Shedd:
>
> Like most families, we have certain unwritten laws that everyone is expected to follow. One of these rules is about our garage door. The last person going to bed is to lock it, and there are no excuses. There has been a great deal of stealing in our neighborhood, and our garage might be very tempting because of the power tools.
>
> One morning recently my husband woke up early, as usual, and went to get the paper. The garage door was wide open. He thought one of the kids had done it and began his usual lecture. But this morning was different. He had just gotten started when Beth, our 15-year-old daughter, stopped him in his tracks with her own lecture.
>
> "Daddy, you left the garage door open. I know you had to be the one because I stayed up late studying, and I certainly locked it when I went to bed. Who else could have done it? Since you weren't home yet, it had to be you! And just in case you wondered, some of us around here have had about all we can take being blamed for things we didn't do!"

Have you ever talked to your father this way? If not, could you? What do you think Beth's father should do?

Mother, I'm Not Supposed to Do Housework!

There aren't too many people who think that housework is great fun. Still, most of us have to do it from time to time. By "housework" I mean everything from doing the dishes to washing the clothes to cooking to sweeping. These are all things that need to be done to keep a house or apartment comfortable and running smoothly.

Felice and Robert are a teenage brother and sister whose opinion of housework is that it's a real drag. For the last year since their parents got divorced, they've been living with their mother. Before the divorce their mom was at home all the time and took care of everything. Nobody else had to lift a finger. Now she goes out to work in a department store during the day, and sometimes she even works nights. There's nothing that

Felice and Robert's mom dislikes more than coming home to a messy living room and a kitchen with dirty dishes left over from dinner. And there's nothing the kids dislike more than housework.

I can understand the kids' point of view. "She's always nagging at us," Felice told me when I talked over the situation with the two of them. Her brother agreed. "The way she goes on," he said, "you'd think that all we're supposed to do is work, work, work! We don't mind if the house is a little messy. It's our house too."

Who do you think is right? The kids who don't like to clean house? Or the mom who doesn't want to come home to a mess? How do you think the family could solve this problem?

Sometimes when there's conflict in a family, the immediate issue (for example, housework) may only be part of the problem. There may be other problems under the surface. In this case I asked all three members of the family how they were feeling about the recent divorce. Naturally, none of them was feeling good about it. A divorce in a family is never a happy event. Felice, Robert, and their mom all agreed that living together as a family of three, with mom working full-time, placed new pressures on all of them. They decided they all needed to be much more considerate of each other.

As a result, Felice and Robert made an extra effort to keep the house as clean and orderly as they could. Of course, they slipped sometimes. The house wasn't always perfect. And their mom tried hard not to expect the house to look just the same as if she were home all the time taking care of it. By trying to understand each other's point of view a little better, this family found solutions to some of its conflicts.

Telephone Rules

The telephone can be a problem, but here's one family that turned it into a good thing. Recently, while I was in their home, an interesting thing happened.

We were sitting by the fire deep in conversation when the 12-year-old daughter came into the room, "Dad," she said, "I've got to make a telephone call. This one will take a while. Do you have any important calls coming in?" When her father had given her the green light, she thanked him and disappeared. I thought that was something special, so I said, "You've got a winner there." To which her dad answered, "Thanks. But actually it's all part of our deal. The telephone used to bug us. So we talked about it and decided on a few rules."

I asked him to tell me more. "When we talked about the telephone," he explained, "everybody had a say. One thing we agreed was that we'd check with each other before a long call." This man is a salesman, and he gets a lot of his orders by phone at home. Too much use of their phone could have been big trouble. But the family handled it by: (1) making some agreements ahead of time and (2) working it out together. What problems at your house could be handled better by some agreements? What could you do to help make things better?

Bicycle Genius

Juan is a genius at fixing bicycles. He has always liked working with his hands. When he started junior high school some of his best friends were working for *A*s. But not Juan. He was taking his bicycle apart and putting it back together. By high school he was making his spending money fixing bicycles.

In school Juan didn't do well because he simply wasn't interested. Nobody would have guessed he'd be like that. His father is a high school social studies teacher, and his mother is a guidance counselor at the same school. But all that stuff wasn't for Juan.

What kind of problem do you think might happen in this situation, where the parents value education and their son couldn't care less? Do you know any family with gaps like this? How do they handle them?

Today Juan owns a bicycle shop. No big deal? It is for Juan. He lives in an area where bicycling is popular, and the thing you may like about all this is what his mother and father said. While Juan was still in high school, they told him, "Juan, we'd really like you to graduate. But we're going to get off your back about grades and a good record and going to college. We're proud of the way you can do things we can't do. More than anything, we want you to be you."

How do your parents allow you to be yourself? Are they understanding? What are you doing to allow the members of your family to be themselves?

Rosemary

Rosemary is a person who makes you feel better knowing her. She isn't a cheerleader or a class officer. Her grades are average. Yet Rosemary is somebody special. She's especially special to Keith.

Keith is her brother, and he's in grade 7. For some people this can be a tough year. Part of you feels old enough to be an adult.

Another part of you still likes to be a kid.

Now, as Keith tries to tackle his problems, here comes Rosemary. Every Sunday afternoon Rosemary takes her brother out for a soft drink or hot chocolate. It's her idea. Of course, she says it's no big deal. But Keith thinks it is.

Is there someone at your house who needs to be listened to? Would someone in your family be healthier if you really cared enough to take him or her aside regularly for the kind of listening and caring you could provide?

A New Family

Everything was okay for 13-year-old Jimmy until his mother got married again. Up to that point he'd had his own room to himself, and he and his mom got along fine.

Jimmy felt happy for his mom when she started to spend time with Gary. But now that Gary is his stepfather, things are different. Gary was part of a package deal that included Gary's two kids from his first marriage. The girl is Jimmy's age; he doesn't like her because he thinks she's a snob. The boy is five years younger, and Jimmy thinks he's a spoiled brat. Worst of all, now that Jimmy's mom and Gary are married, Jimmy has to share a room in their new house with his stepbrother.

Many families today are made up of stepbrothers and stepsisters. It's not so unusual. And because it involves a change from how things used to be, it takes some getting used to. What could Jimmy do to improve the situation with his new sister and brother? What could the whole family do together to make things better?

II. Getting Along with Your Parents

As you can see from all these examples, there are many potential sore spots between parents and their children: money, chores, clothes, hair, homework, friends, and lots of others. In fact, almost anything you mention could be a battleground. This can be especially true in families that are going through certain kinds of stress that are common in families today.

It's even more important when your family is under stress for you to think about their needs and to be extra careful of each others' feelings. Otherwise, problems and conflicts are bound to arise.

From what I've learned watching my own kids, and from the families I've seen who were getting the job done, I've put together these "Twelve Rules for Getting Along with Your Parents."

1. *Remember, there are times when you're no bargain to live with either!*

   If there is one thing as tough as being a teenager, it's having one. So when things get rough between you and your folks, suppose you go straight down the hall and look in the mirror. You'll do a great thing for your future if you learn to start thinking about your "people" problems by asking the question "When am *I* wrong?"

2. *You can't always get everything you want. There are other people in the world besides you!*

   You're at the age when you begin wanting more. You want to try new ideas, to feel more grown-up, to impress more people. But maybe you had better back off now and then to see the whole picture. Your family wants what's best for you. And they may be right, even if you can't see it.

3. *Let others have their way sometimes, especially with the little things.*

   The wise teenager doesn't try to win every argument. If you show your parents you're willing to give at times, you're being smart. They'll be more likely to cooperate when it's some big deal that you really care about.

4. *Show a little sympathy.*

   Trying to be understanding is a good start for improving any relationship. What it means is that you try to see things through the other person's eyes.

5. *Make a sincere vow to say "thank you" to family members at least once every day.*

   Saying "thanks" is an important key to building respect for one another. It will give you a sense of pride by making family members feel good and will help them feel appreciated for their efforts to be good parents.

6. *At least once a week do something nice for family members.*

Any little thing will do, as long as they weren't expecting it and you get the message across that you'd like to make life a little easier for them. I know one girl who, during her teenage years, would say to her parents now and then, "This Friday I'm going to stay home and baby-sit. You're going out and have a good time." What do you suppose that did for their feelings toward her?

7. *Never do anything to betray their trust or make them question your honesty.*

The first time you lie to your parents, you have put your foot on a dangerous road. It may be difficult to understand this until you are a parent. When your family loses faith in you and it's your fault, you have lost more than you want to lose.

8. *To avoid some arguments, make a few agreements in advance.*

   Ahead of time you can settle some questions, such as: Where can you go? What time will you be in? How much allowance will you get? What work will you do around the house? How much privacy will they give you? Dozens of things can be settled in advance, rather than fought over later. Smart teenagers think ahead.

9. *Ask for your parents' advice now and then on something big enough to make them feel important.*

   There isn't a parent alive who wouldn't react favorably to the four words "I need your help." Parents really do know some things worth knowing. They would be flattered. And would that ever improve feelings around home!

10. *Tell your parents you'd like to know about sex straight from them.*

    So they were brought up in a day when things were different. But they must know a little. If you'd only ask them, or listen long enough, or keep a straight face long enough, maybe it wouldn't be half bad. And the way I'd begin would be something like this: "I know you're a lot smarter than some of the people who have been telling me about sex. Will you answer some questions for me?"

11. *Learn to talk and listen.*

    Yelling, pouting, and running to your room in anger are not ways to improve your relationship with your parents. Just as you learn to accept and adjust to your friends, the same is true about your parents. You need to accept them and make adjustments for your differences. This probably won't happen without some honest and open talking—and listening.

12. *Learn how to disagree.*

    Expect some disagreement. Don't be ashamed of anger. It's a natural part of being a thinking person. The only thing you need to regret is when you handle it badly. Learn how to keep your cool during a disagreement by staying in control and not raising your voice. Learn how to compromise. And, above all, learn these four words: "I'm sorry. I apologize."

Think about which of these rules you'd like to use in your family right away. And think about which ones might be more difficult for your family to use. Better still, make up some rules of your own. It's never too late to start. Choosing to get along better with your family is the most important decision you'll ever make. Good luck!

No Party for Nancy

a short story by
Hank Resnik

Nancy could tell by the light under her parents' bedroom door that they were still awake. Very quietly she knocked.

She could hear her mother's voice. "Jack, did you hear something?"

Then she heard her father mumble, "Hmm?" He sounded half asleep. She could picture the scene. Her father had turned off the TV after watching the ten o'clock news, and her mother was still studying her law books. Since her mother had started law school, she was always studying.

Nancy knocked again.

"Yes?" her mother called. "Is that you, Nancy?"

"Can I talk to you a minute?" Nancy said.

"Come on in," her mother said.

Sure enough, her mother was propped up in bed on two pillows with a book in her hand, and her father was lying on his side. Her mother peered at Nancy over her little half-glasses. "What is it, Nancy?" she said.

"I'm sorry," Nancy said. "Am I disturbing you? You're studying."

"No, that's all right. Did you want to talk about something?"

Nancy was annoyed with herself for finding all this so difficult. "I . . . I just wondered if you and Dad have plans for Saturday night."

"We're going out to dinner with the Jacksons," Nancy's father mumbled.

"Yes," Nancy's mother said. "Why do you want to know?"

Nancy's fingers traced an aimless pattern on the bedspread. "I just wondered." Realizing how weak this sounded, she rushed on. "Claudia invited me over to her house. I thought if you were going out you'd feel better if I wasn't alone. I could go to Claudia's."

Nancy's father sat up in bed now. "Who will be at Claudia's?" he asked. His voice was full of clouds and far-off rumbles of thunder.

"Nobody, really," Nancy said. Boy, was she making a mess of this! "Just a few kids."

"And Claudia's parents?" her mother asked. Looking at Nancy from over the tops of her half-glasses, she could have been a judge.

"I'm not sure," Nancy said. She was thinking she'd better stop before she told one more lie. They were little lies, but they were lies.

Her father's voice was surprisingly calm. "Nancy, you know what the rule is. No overnights or night visiting unless it's been arranged with the other child's parents."

"I'm not a child!" Nancy felt close to tears.

"You only just turned 13," Nancy's father said.

"Let's not start this discussion again," said Nancy's mother. "Nancy, you know what the rules are. We'd be happy to talk with Claudia's parents about Saturday night. Just get one of them on the phone."

"It isn't fair," Nancy nearly shouted. "No one else my age has to go through this. You check on every little move I make!"

"A party on a Saturday night isn't a little move," Nancy's mother said. "Your father and I have heard about these parties."

"Well, the other kids are allowed to go to them," Nancy said. "The other parents don't boss their kids around like police."

"Maybe you don't want us talking with Claudia's parents," her father said, "because there's something about Saturday night you don't want us to know. I hope not, but that's what it sounds like. Now, we're not going to discuss this again until you make that phone call."

Nancy turned and left the room without a word. As she walked down the hall, she mumbled to herself, "I'm never allowed to have any fun."

She paused at the door to her own room long enough to hear her mother saying, "I don't know what she's hiding, but she's hiding something. She's never been sneaky before. I don't like it."

Well, Mrs. Policewoman, Nancy thought to herself. You haven't seen anything yet.

Usually Claudia got to school early to spend time with her friends. Standing on the top step, Nancy searched the crowd in the schoolyard, holding a hand up to her eyes to shield them from the morning sun.

Suddenly she heard a voice saying, "I know. You're Columbus discovering America, except you're lost."

Nancy turned to face her friend. "Where've you been?" she said. "I've been looking all over for you."

"Like Columbus said—I've been around," Claudia answered. She was famous for not taking anything seriously.

"Claudia, I can't go," Nancy said. "They won't let me."

"You asked them?"

"It didn't get that far. I started to ask them, and they told me the rule is that they have to talk to 'the other child's' parent."

Claudia snickered. " 'The other child.' Your parents are a gas."

Nancy snickered too. "Yeah, a real gas."

"So what are you going to do?"

"I can't have them call your mother. If they find out you're having the party while your parents are away, they'll probably move to another town or something so I won't be contaminated by you."

Claudia took a small compact from her purse, opened it, and inspected her reflection in its mirror. "Well, I'm sorry you won't be there," she said. "Last night I talked with this guy I know in the high school, and he said he's going to bring a bunch of the cutest boys. And some of them have their own cars. One of them is buying a keg. It'll be a blast."

Nancy's eyes opened wide. "Gee, what if your parents find out?"

Claudia snapped her compact shut and returned it to her purse. "The difference between my parents and your parents," she said, "is, number one, they won't find out, and, number two, it wouldn't be any big deal if they did."

Nancy felt as if a huge mound of sadness was pressing in on her. "You're so lucky," she said. "I wish I had parents like yours."

"Well, you won't always be living with your parents," Claudia said, "and they won't always be bossing you around. Look at the bright side."

Nancy felt like crying. "Yeah, look at the bright side. Only five more years. Unless I drop out of school. And then what would I do?"

Claudia seemed far away and superior. "We'll miss you at the party, kid," she said. "Really. I'm sorry."

Nancy took a big breath. "You don't need to feel sorry for me," she said. "I'm going to be there. I wouldn't miss this party for anything."

Saturday morning at Nancy's house was always a time for routines. It was a time for her father to have what he called "his time"—as opposed to "his time with Nancy," "his time with Mom," or "everybody's time together." This morning he'd already left the house. Her mother, Nancy knew, would be going shopping.

Nancy's routine was to do her chores. It seemed that every year there were newer and harder ones—vacuuming the living room and the stairs, cleaning her own room, doing laundry. Sometimes she wondered if her parents spent their spare time dreaming up new chores for her to do.

Nancy's plan for today included her chores, as usual. Of course. She didn't want things to seem too different. But this was a special Saturday, the Saturday of Claudia's party. One routine she had no intention of following today was the "Nancy goody-goody who never does anything she isn't supposed to and never has any fun" routine. She would do her chores, but she had other things in mind.

She launched Phase One of her plan as soon as her mother left the house to go shopping. With the vacuum cleaner running, Nancy watched from her bedroom window as her mother got into her car and drove away. After the car had turned the corner, the first thing Nancy did was turn on the radio full blast. Playing loud music wasn't the main part of the plan, but it was something she was never allowed to do.

Then Nancy rushed to the linen closet in the hall, where she knew some spare pillows were kept. She dashed back to her room with two of them and grabbed her old teddy bear from her own closet. Only a year ago Nancy had decided that she was too old to sleep with the bear, so she'd put it on the closet shelf. Today it would be useful again.

The two pillows fit nicely under the bedcovers. Then Nancy placed the teddy bear so that its head rested on her pillow. She pulled the sheet and blanket over the bear's head and stepped back. Perfect! Anyone who looked in from the doorway would swear it was Nancy sleeping there.

Nancy did a little dance to the blaring music. She could picture the party now. Older boys . . . beer . . . . She'd never tasted beer before, but she knew she would love it. She could see it all now. She'd be nice little goody-goody Nancy right up to dinner time. Then she and her mother would fix something for her to eat, and her mother would sit and chat with her at the kitchen table while she had her dinner. Then, she'd go in to the den to watch TV, and her mother would go upstairs. A while later, both of her parents would come down all dressed up and smelling nice. They'd give her a kiss and a hug on their way out of the house and say, "Be a good girl. Don't stay up too late."

Tonight would be different. Tonight she would be going out too. Nancy closed her eyes as she swayed to the beat of the music and imagined that a cute boy at the party was asking her to share a beer with him. Tonight would be different. . . .

"Nancy! What is going on here! That music is so loud I could hear it halfway down the block!"

Nancy's mother was standing at the bedroom door, her mouth open in astonishment.

Nancy could feel her blood going cold. For a moment she considered falling, sort of, onto her bed so her mother couldn't see what she'd done to it. But she realized that it was too late. It was clear that her mother saw. And she could tell that her mother understood.

"Turn that radio off," Nancy's mother said.

Nancy went over to the desk, turned off the radio, and then sat on the bed.

The silence was terrible. Her mother walked over to the bed and looked down at it, then pulled the sheet and blanket back to reveal the head of the teddy bear on the pillow. "Obviously, you didn't expect me to forget my wallet and have to come back so soon," her mother said. "You were going to go to Claudia's party, weren't you?"

Nancy nodded.

"Your father said he thought you might try something like this. He must know you better than I do." Suddenly her mother straightened up and looked very determined. "Come with me, Nancy."

Nancy followed her mother across the hall to her parents' room and stood watching as she jabbed angrily at the buttons on the bedside telephone. "Hello, Shirley?" her mother said into the phone. "This is Ann. Something has come up, and Jack and I won't be able to have dinner with you and Richard tonight. I'm awfully sorry too. We need to be with Nancy tonight. I'll tell you more about it when I see you. Let's do it another time. 'Bye, dear.''

Nancy stood there, feeling numb. Nothing like this had ever happened before.

"Go ahead and finish your chores," her mother finally said. "We'll talk about this when your father gets home."

Nancy turned and started toward the door but stopped at the sound of her mother's voice.

"Nancy!" Her mother's eyes were searching hers. "I always thought I could trust you. I never doubted it. Now I'm beginning to wonder."

Sometimes Nancy found her family so boring and predictable that she could hardly stand it. Sunday mornings were typical of this. If the family wasn't away on one of their trips, almost every Sunday of the year they read the comics from the newspaper together. They'd been doing it ever since Nancy could remember. It used to be fun. But now it seemed so childish. Because of it she was reluctant to invite other girls for Saturday sleepovers.

This Sunday morning was especially difficult. Everyone, it seemed, was in a bad mood. The main thing her parents had decided when they all talked the day before was that Nancy hadn't actually done anything, so a punishment wasn't appropriate. Nancy was on notice, though, that her parents would be supervising her much more closely than before. Nancy didn't see how that was possible.

They were halfway through the comics, and everybody had had at least one turn at reading when the phone rang. Nancy's mother went to answer it in the front hallway. "Well, hello, Janice," she said. "How nice to hear from you. We were just relaxing. The three of us. Nancy. She's 13 now. Yes. She's fine. Why? Claudia Morton? Yes, Claudia's a friend of Nancy's. What! When? Good heavens! Why, that's terrible! Where were the parents? Is she going to be all right? Oh, that's terrible! You hear about this kind of thing, but you always think it only happens to other people. It could have been Nancy."

At this point Nancy's mother's voice became much quieter. Soon afterwards she came back into the room, a worried frown on her face.

"What happened?" asked Nancy's father.

"That was Janice Phillips," Nancy's mother said. "She lives across the street from the Mortons—over on Hill Drive. I guess she knew that Nancy and Claudia are friends . . . ." She sat down on the sofa. "There was a very serious automobile accident last night," she said. "One of the boys from the party had a bunch of kids in the car. He'd been drinking. The car went off the road. Several kids were hurt."

"Is Claudia all right?" asked Nancy. Her heart was beating very fast.

"Claudia is in the hospital. Sloan Hospital. Her parents are away for the weekend. Her uncle is looking after her until they get home." Suddenly her tone was louder, angry. "That's nice, isn't it? They're away for the weekend while their daughter's in the hospital." But she stopped herself. Nancy's parents always said that the way other people raised their children was no one else's business.

Nancy hated the smell of hospitals. She'd been waiting for hours, it seemed, before finally a nurse in a spotless white uniform appeared and called her name. Nancy stood up, and the nurse smiled at her. "You're here to see Claudia Morton?"

"Yes."

"She's still tired after the operation, but you can visit for a few minutes. I'm sure she'll be glad to see you."

The nurse led Nancy down a long corridor and into a room with two beds. One of them was empty. The other contained a figure that appeared to be completely covered by bandages and casts. Nancy recognized Claudia's bright blue eyes and brown hair.

"Claudia, look at you," Nancy exclaimed. "Good heavens!"

"You think this would make it in a fashion show?" Claudia's voice sounded distant and slightly hollow, as if she were speaking inside a tunnel.

"Oh, Claudia! Good heavens!"

"Stop that. It's bad enough without your 'good heavenses.'"

"Are . . . are you all right?" Nancy stammered.

"Yeah, I'm okay. I guess."

"What about your parents? What did they say?"

"They called me from the ski lodge where they're staying, and they said my uncle is in charge of everything and they'll see me when they get home tomorrow night." Claudia's eyes closed, and Nancy just stood there, gaping. "They made the reservations months ago. It's this very fancy place, and they have a waiting list just to stay there."

"I wish I'd been at the party," Nancy said. "Maybe it wouldn't have happened if I'd been there."

"That's ridiculous," Claudia said. Nancy could see that tears were welling up in her eyes and starting to roll down her cheeks into the bandages that covered most of her head. "Besides, it was a lousy party."

"I could kill my mother," Nancy said. "She found out what I was going to do, and they stopped me. I was going to go. I had it all worked out. I keep thinking that if I'd only been there . . . ."

Claudia's eyes were closing, and she seemed exhausted. "Believe me," she mumbled. "It was a lousy party. You didn't miss a thing. You don't know how lucky you are."

Star  ters

No question about it—getting along with our families can be a real challenge. Some days everything seems okay, and other days it feels like a war zone. But that's normal. The key is to help make family relationships as good as they can be. Create more sunshine than thunder. Here are some suggestions for improving the home "climate":

★ Everyone in your family deserves respect—just like you.

★ Everyone in your family needs love, kindness, and appreciation—just like you.

★ Always be honest. It's the best way to build trust in your family.

★ To build good relations with parents, brothers, and sisters, begin by putting yourself in their shoes. Treat them as you would like to be treated.

★ All families have their good qualities. Focus on the good things in your family.

127

Decisions

Part 6

"If I was in a situation where people were using drugs and alcohol, I probably wouldn't know what to do."

"My brother got really messed up on drugs. It scares me to see what drugs can do to people. My brother had to go live in a special place for people with drug problems for more than a year, and now that he's out of there he doesn't know what to do with his life. He doesn't have anything to take the place of drugs."

"It just seems incredible that some kids think smoking is cool. Smoking is so gross and disgusting! The smell of it alone makes me angry because it makes me start choking. It's amazing the tobacco companies manage to stay in business."

"Everywhere you look there's some kind of ad showing people who are just so cool and glamorous or rich or something, and they're smoking and drinking. But then your parents tell you not to smoke and drink because it's bad for you. I don't know what to think!"

"A few of the kids at my school smoke marijuana in the bathroom. It's the group that's always in trouble. I don't even talk to them."

"I went to a party where there were some older kids drinking beer. I couldn't believe how much beer they were drinking. Toward the end of the party some of them were getting really sick and throwing up. It sure didn't look like fun to me!"

We live in a world in which many different kinds of chemical substances—alcohol, cigarettes, and other drugs—are widely abused. Why do people use drugs? Often they think that drugs will make them feel better—or be better. The problem is, though, that when people decide to use drugs they're taking a huge risk. They're risking their health and sometimes even their lives.

This section was written entirely by Peggy Mann, a nationally known expert on drugs and youth. The article, "Facts for Healthier Decisions: Getting Straight on Alcohol, Tobacco, and Marijuana," provides you with important information about the most commonly used chemical substances. These facts should be the basis for any decision you make about alcohol, tobacco, and marijuana. Peggy Mann knows how to present them in a way that's easy to understand.

The short story, "Being Cool," shows why one girl almost falls into the trap of drug use. Angie is the new girl in town, and the main thing she wants when she starts her first day in school is a friend—any friend. For a while it seems that she's even willing to settle for friends who spend a lot of time using drugs. It's a terrible conflict for Angie. Fortunately, her mom helps her deal with the conflict—and be true to herself.

Facts for Healthier Decisions: Getting Straight on Alcohol, Tobacco and Marijuana

by
Peggy Mann

"That's impossible!" I said to the editor. "You want me to write about the harmful effects of cigarettes, alcohol, marijuana, and other drugs—all in eight pages?"

"Well...." His voice sounded a little faint. Was this because of the long-distance telephone, or because he knew that what he was asking *was* impossible?

"Have you seen the *Report of the U.S. Surgeon General on Smoking and Health?*" I asked. "It's the fattest book I own. It has over 2,000 pages of summaries of 30,000 research papers on the harmful effects of cigarettes on different parts of the body.

"I have a paper from Canadian government and health officials that says 30,000 people die each year in Canada because of tobacco-related illnesses.

"Now—how many pages are you giving me on cigarette smoking?"

"Well," said the editor, "maybe—two?"

"Two? And how about pot?" Before he could answer, I rushed on. "I have on my shelf four books with over 6,000 summaries of published papers written by scientists since 1979.

They show the harm marijuana can do to the lungs, the brain, the sex organs, the reproductive system, the immune system, and the babies of pot-smoking mothers. Not to mention the harm it does to the personality of the pot smoker." I paused. "Now—how many pages are you giving me for marijuana?"

"All right," he said, "since so many kids still think pot is harmless, how about—five pages?"

"And alcohol? And uppers, downers, lookalikes, speed, and the whole alphabet soup of drugs like PCP and LSD—am I to cover them all in one page?"

He sighed. "Okay, divide up the sections any way you want—in a total of 13 pages."

Well, at least I'd gotten a few extra pages! I'll do my best in this short space to pick out what may be most important to you about cigarettes, alcohol, and pot. But remember, what you'll be reading here is only the tip of a very large—and dangerous—iceberg.

Alcohol, Drugs—and Driving

The fact that the "iceberg" is dangerous is clearly shown in another U.S. Surgeon General's report. It has a cheerful title: *Healthy People.* And most of the things it has to say are cheerful. Because of many of the giant steps in medicine, the death rate for babies, children through the age of 14, and grownups over the age of 26 is lower than it was for their age groups 25 years ago.

But there is one age group in which the death rate has risen: 15-24-year olds. Many more people in this age group are dying than was true of the same age group 25 years ago. And what do you think is the main cause of this rise in the death rate? The Surgeon General's report calls it "driving mixed with substances." What are "substances"? That's the name often given to alcohol and drugs. (Further evidence of how dangerous these chemicals can be is that the second reason for deaths in this age group is alcohol- and drug-related suicides and accidents that don't involve driving.)

Since I said that in these 13 pages I would pick out what I thought might be most important to you, and since most of you reading this chapter won't be old enough to have a driver's license, why start with the subject of alcohol, drugs, and driving? Here's why: have you ever ridden in a car driven by a teenager who'd been smoking a joint or who'd had a few beers or popped a few pills? Or all three?

Maybe you haven't—yet. But unless you're very different from most kids, the time will come when someone who is "under the influence" will say, "Come on. Get in. I'll drive you."

It's not easy to say "No thanks." But the graph on this page may help you. Do you see how the death rate caused by car crashes shoots up for teenagers? Drivers aren't the only ones killed. The death rate of passengers starts zooming up at about the age of 13. And the death rate for kids who are passengers stays just as high as the death rate for teenage drivers!

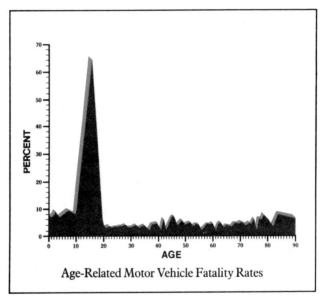

Age-Related Motor Vehicle Fatality Rates

A lot of young people and adults say, "I'd never ride in a car driven by someone who's been drinking. But I feel safe with a pot smoker." Well, more than 75 research studies have clearly shown that marijuana is just as harmful to the driver as alcohol, although sometimes in different ways. A driver under the influence of marijuana means a dangerous driver. Pot plus alcohol means double trouble, and many pot smokers drink while they "toke."

Another danger is this: the most important new study done on alcohol, marijuana, and driving shows that a half-hour after the pot-smoking subjects "came down" from the high, they were in worse shape than when they were stoned. And in some of the tests, the pot smokers were more impaired than the alcohol drinkers.

Half the traffic deaths each year are alcohol-related. No one knows how many more deaths are drug-related because no one has looked carefully at those statistics. The important thing for you to remember is: don't risk being a statistic. Don't worry about insulting the driver. Worry about your own safety, your own life. Phone home and ask for a lift. Borrow bus or taxi money. Or walk. Every year many thousands of kids your age die in car crashes. Many hundreds of thousands are injured. All of us like to think that these things only happen to the other guy, "not to me." Well, remember, all those kids who were injured or killed in a car crash thought that too!

Now, in the space that's left, let's look at the three "substances" you'll be offered most often, starting with the one many kids don't consider a drug at all.

Alcohol

A bottle of beer or a glass of wine—a drug? Yes, alcohol is a drug. For drugs—at least the kind we're talking about in this chapter—are mind-altering substances. And alcohol can be mind-altering. In fact, that's the reason most kids drink: to get sloshed, clobbered, sozzled, smashed, bombed, plastered—drunk.

On the other hand, most adults do not drink to get drunk. In fact, one-third don't drink alcohol at all, and another one-third drink only a little. A glass of wine at dinner. A beer when watching a ball game on TV. A cocktail at a party—but just one; after that it's a soft drink.

When you drink one can of beer, you're getting as much of the drug ethyl alcohol as when you drink one glass of wine or a shot of whiskey. All three contain the same amount of ethyl alcohol. Rubbing alcohol has nothing whatever to do with ethyl alcohol. Some kids get confused because the name's the same. But rubbing alcohol is poison. Drinking even a little can make you very sick. A lot can kill you. But no amount will get you high.

There are other important things for kids your age to remember about alcohol:

1. The smaller and thinner you are, the faster you'll get drunk and the drunker you'll get.

2. Many teenagers "chug-a-lug" beer—drink it down as fast as they can, sometimes without a breath. This is very dangerous. Kids have overdosed and ended up in the hospital due to drinking too much too fast.

3. "Upchucking" is the body's natural way of getting rid of too much alcohol. But kids who smoke pot and drink alcohol often don't vomit, because pot "turns off" the vomit center of the brain. Instead, they may overdose.

4. People often refer to alcohol as "our legal drug." Not many stop to point out that it is also an illegal drug for young people under the age of 21—depending on the laws in your state or province. Lawmakers made it illegal for a sound and simple reason: they are looking out for your health.

5. Alcohol can be addictive—which means when you drink a lot, your body and mind keep craving more and more. An estimated three million teenagers are problem drinkers. Alcohol causes them problems of all sorts—problems with school, with their friends, with their families, and with their health. One of the biggest problems is that, without special help, they just can't stop drinking.

Cigarettes

Some people call cigarettes a drug; some don't. But everyone agrees on one thing: cigarettes are one of the most addictive substances there are. So, from that point of view, cigarettes are a drug.

"Drug" is a strange word. The kinds of drugs you take when you're sick should really be called "medications." If you take them as they're prescribed by a doctor, they can help you get well. But the kinds of drugs we're talking about in this chapter have two things in common: (1) they can be addictive; (2) they're bad for you.

With only a few short pages, there's no space to even begin to describe the different ways in which cigarettes can harm you. Instead, I'll mention three points you may find of interest:

1. About 50 years ago lung cancer among women was almost unheard of. And at that time for women to smoke was almost unheard of. Today, with women smoking almost as much as men—and young women more heavily than young men—lung cancer among women almost equals the rate for men. If you ask why, we know of only one clear reason: cigarette smoking.

    Lungs are only one of the organs harmed by cigarettes. And lung cancer is only one of the ways in which the lungs are harmed. Cigarettes are also linked with heart disease. In short, cigarettes are one of the leading killers we know about.

2. Here's a demonstration you can try yourself. Ask a smoker to blow a puff of cigarette smoke into a white handkerchief stretched across his or her mouth. You'll see a small, round, yellowish-brown stain. Now, imagine the smoker blowing 15 to 20 puffs into the handkerchief. It would be dotted with round, brownish stains. And that's from only one cigarette. Imagine all the stains on the handkerchief from a pack of

20 cigarettes. And from a pack a day for a week. A month. A year! By that time you'd have to hold up a handkerchief the size of a sheet! Obviously, in the case of the smoker, the tars and nicotine making all those stains do not go harmlessly into a white handkerchief—but into the lungs.

Imagine if a factory opened up next door to your house and the chimney blew polluted smoke straight into your bedroom window. You and your family would soon be out picketing. You'd have newspapers and TV covering the story—everyone would be furious at the factory. Your anger and your message would be heard: "Stop polluting my room. It's bad for my health." But who can hear your lungs, your heart, and other organs when they protest pollution from cigarette smoke?

They're being harmed, however. That's why cigarette smoking is the largest cause of preventable death today. Smoking, for example, contributes to one in every three cancer deaths every year. The ads may make smoking look cool, but medical experts have described it as "slow motion suicide."

3. A 1983 study of 13-17-year-olds showed that the cigarette smokers were less athletic than the nonsmokers. They read less and got lower grades. Also, they drank far more coffee and alcohol, and they smoked pot far more than those who did not smoke tobacco cigarettes. Local and national surveys show that kids who start early drinking beer or smoking tobacco cigarettes are far more likely to go on to pot than those who don't smoke cigarettes or drink. As my daughter, who's now 20, summed up, "All of these things were 'in' when I was growing up. But now more and more kids feel that cigarette smoking is disgusting. And they also feel that being smashed or stoned is tacky and gross."

All of which brings us to—

The Problems of Pot

Many people continue to think that marijuana is a harmless substance. Nothing could be further from the truth. There are four main reasons for this:

1. Many kids think of marijuana as a simple, harmless weed. In fact, marijuana contains 421 chemicals, the most dangerous being a chemical called "THC." It harms your brain cells, your reproductive system, your lungs, and your body's built-in system to fight disease and infections.

2. Marijuana has almost the same harmful chemicals that tobacco has. In fact, some of the most harmful chemicals are found in 50 to 100 percent greater amounts in pot smoke.

3. In addition, marijuana has 61 harmful chemicals found only in the cannabis plant—from which pot, hashish, and hash oil are produced. These chemicals are called cannabinoids. They are unlike chemicals in tobacco and other drugs because they are lipophilic. Lipo means "fat." Philic means "loving."

   Instead of washing out of the body as other chemicals do, the fat-loving cannabinoids seek out and seep into the fatty sections of the cells. They collect in the fatty organs. The brain, for example, is one-third fat. (As one scientist told me: "From that point of view we're all fatheads.") The sex organs (the ovaries and testicles) are also very fatty.

   Only very slowly do the cannabinoids leak back out into the bloodstream and leave the body through the urine and feces. One of Canada's pioneer marijuana researchers, Dr. Alexander Jakubovic, has pointed out that the cannabinoids take a week or two, or even longer, to clear out of the body. If a person smokes more than one joint a week, the cannabinoids in the second joint add to those in the first. And the body is never drug-free.

   This is why marijuana affects the entire body, from the smallest cells up to the highest levels of life—the mind and the personality.

139

4. Marijuana is an intoxicant. And "toxic" means poison. Therefore, even when the regular pot smoker is not high, harmful chemicals are collecting throughout his or her body.

What does this collection of cannabinoids do? When people ask me this, I sometimes say, "Pick an organ." Many people pick the lungs. And I tell them about the studies showing that pot smokers have the same harmful lung symptoms that are found in tobacco smokers, but the symptoms come on faster. The only harmful "cigarette lung symptom" that hasn't shown up yet is lung cancer. Many experts point out, though, that it takes 30 or 40 years for lung cancer to develop. Studies of regular pot smokers have been going on just for the last 15 or 20 years.

Sometimes when I say "Pick an organ," people pick the sex organs. And I tell them about new findings showing the harmful effects on babies of pot-smoking fathers or mothers.

But when I say, "Pick an organ," most people pick the brain. After all, you smoke pot to get high, to have your brain "altered." So they want to know how marijuana changes the brain—and if these changes harm the brain.

The scientist who has done the most work on pot and brain cell changes is Dr. Robert Heath, of Tulane University Medical School. He used rhesus monkeys for his studies. Some kids "turn off" when they hear this. They say, "I'm not a monkey—so the results don't matter to me." But for brain cell studies, monkeys make better subjects than humans.

Suppose a known pot smoker were killed in a car crash and his brain cells were examined under the microscope—and abnormal changes were found. You could never be sure that the changes weren't caused by other drugs, or alcohol, or some illness the person has had.

But Dr. Heath knew his monkey subjects since they were born. None had been sick. None had been given any drugs. All had the same diet.

He divided them into three groups for his experiment. Some of them were exposed to pot smoke, and some weren't. After six months all exposure to pot smoke was stopped for another six months. Then Dr. Heath examined the brain cells of the monkeys in the three different groups. He found that:

1. The brain cells of the group that hadn't been exposed to any pot smoke were perfectly normal.

2. The second group was exposed to pot smoke equal to two joints one-fourth the size of a normal joint, two days a week, for six months. The brain cells of the monkeys in this group were beginning to show abnormalities. (Abnormal means that something is wrong.)

3. The third group Dr. Heath called "The Heavy Smokers." These monkeys were exposed to pot smoke equal to two joints a day, five days a week, for six months. Almost all the brain cells the scientist looked at in this group were abnormal. And he looked at many hundreds of brain cells. Some were more abnormal than others. For example, most had dark, swollen clots usually found only in very old monkeys or humans. But these were all young monkeys.

When Dr. Heath looked at the damage pot had done to the monkeys' brain cells, he began to understand why many of the heavy pot-smoking human patients he saw had the same symptoms. Their memories were bad. They felt people were "out to get them." They were often irritable and depressed. And they cared less and less about things in their lives that had once interested them: sports, music, their families—everything except getting and smoking pot.

On the next page is a picture of brain cells from a "heavy smoker." The difference between the two cells is that one was exposed to THC and the other was not.

First look at the picture on the left—it looks like a perfectly normal cell. The little round blobs hold chemical activators of the brain. That's how everything we think, feel, or do is passed on in the brain.

Now look at the picture on the right. The little blobs are all clumped together. This makes it harder for them to spill their chemical activators, and it further slows down the movement of messages in the brain. It may also affect memory.

Dr. Heath realized that all the "pot personality" changes he had seen in his heavy pot-smoking patients could well have been caused by the brain cell abnormalities brought about by pot smoke. Of course, it's true that people aren't monkeys. But cells in the section of the brain examined by Dr. Heath are so similar to human brain cells that under the microscope it's impossible to tell the difference. According to Dr. Heath, it's wishful thinking to hope that what happened to the monkeys' brain cells does not happen in humans.

The good news is that Dr. Heath and others working with "pot personality" patients report that when teenagers cut out pot completely—which means never taking another joint—

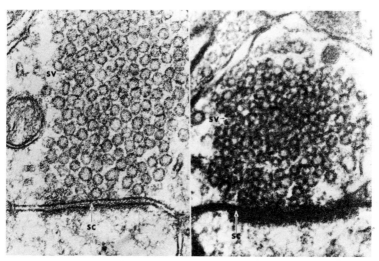

Left: brain cell from rhesus monkey exposed to pot smoke with the THC removed.

Right: typical impaired brain cell of monkey exposed to same amount of pot smoke with THC.

From *Marijuana Alert*, by Peggy Mann. New York: McGraw-Hill, 1984, p. 180.

they seem to "get it back together again." Adults also improve. But they often complain that their memory isn't what it was before they began pot smoking.

One thing is certain. Pot—still thought by many kids to be harmless—is, in fact, extremely harmful in many ways. Some of the ways may not show on the surface. But countless studies clearly reveal that the harm is going on slowly but surely in many organs of the body.

Another thing is certain. If you haven't already been offered a joint, you probably will be offered one in the future. And not just once but maybe many times. ("Come on, try it. One isn't going to hurt you. You'll like it. It feels great.")

Most kids like to try different things. And in some schools kids who smoke dope are still looked at as "cool."

So—why not?

The trouble is this: after that first joint, it's even harder to say "No" to the second—and the third. Nothing bad seems to be happening to you. So why not? Just one more.

Well, here are two things to think about—hard.

1. Surveys of students age 12 and older show that one-third of those who have ever used marijuana (and that includes "trying just one joint") become daily users at some point in their lives.

2. The National High School Senior Survey taken in the U.S. shows that of those who smoke pot at all during the year, about half also use other illegal drugs. The half who don't smoke pot use virtually no other illegal drugs.

Well, my page limit is up. And I haven't said a word about uppers, downers, and the other illegal drugs. But I can cover them all in one short sentence. None of them will do you any good; all of them will do you harm.

There's one simple word that will make life much easier and healthier for you when you're offered alcohol and drugs. So I'll end this chapter with it.

Just say "No."

"The best way to escape from a problem is to solve it."

145

Being Cool

a short story by
Peggy Mann

Angie walked up the stone steps very slowly. It was the first day of school after the summer vacation—which was hard enough. But for Angie it was a triple first. Her first day at a new school in a new town that she hated. Sommerville! For someone who had lived until the age of almost-13 in a big city, to be suddenly moved to a stupid, nowhere place like Sommerville was . . . the end. And here, in Endsville she had to try to make all new beginnings.

On the school steps kids were running up and down to greet each other, flinging their arms around each other, all excited about meeting after the summer vacation. Others were going through the school doors arm in arm or standing around in little groups talking. Everyone was with someone. She was the only one all alone.

She entered the school building. The walls were painted white and were brightly lit, a far cry from the olive-green color of the school she had gone to in the city. But what she wouldn't give now to be walking through those dim, dingy halls—with her friends!

Her homeroom was 3-B. But she couldn't face going in there to spend 20 long minutes until the first period began—watching, as everyone greeted everyone else. She wished her dad had been considerate enough—this first day anyhow—to drop her off just before school started. But, of course, he had to get to his new job at Gardners on time, which had meant dropping Angie off early.

She passed a door that said "Girls" and gratefully went in. At least here it wouldn't show, her being all alone.

Inside the restroom another girl stood by the mirror, brushing her hair. "Hi," she said. Angie said "Hi" back. Maybe she could quickly turn this new girl into a friend. She took a deep breath and said in one gulp of a sentence, "My name is Angie Bellock. I'm from the city. I'm new in the school and in this town. What's yours? Your name, I mean."

The girl stopped brushing her hair and looked at Angie. She seemed to be looking her over. As if she were measuring her in some way. Then she said, "My name is Gene. Spelled with a 'G.' It's really Eugenia. But everyone calls me Gene—with a 'G.' My friends sometimes call me Gigi."

"Oh," Angie said. "Should I?"

"Should you what?"

"Call you Gigi."

The girl shrugged. Then she said, "Sure." She giggled,

though Angie couldn't see what was so funny. Then Gigi took some eyedrops out of her bookbag, tilted her head back, and put several drops into each eye. "God bless Visine!" Then she asked, "Do you party?"

Angie nodded. If she said she didn't party she'd lose this perhaps-friend before they even got started.

"I guess in a big place like the city," Gigi said, "they have a lot more fun. I've been to the city a couple of times. It's exciting. Not like here. Believe me, they got the name wrong—this is Deadsville."

Angie nodded, wondering what to say next and hoping she wouldn't make a mistake. "We moved here last week because my Dad was made the new manager of Gardners," she said. "He was the assistant manager of their branch in the city. He thought being manager here would be a good opportunity for him. So we moved. Have you ever been to Gardners?"

"Sure," said Gigi. "It's the best clothing store in the shopping center. You're lucky. Do you get clothes for free?"

"No," said Angie. "But my mom and I do get discounts." She started brushing her hair, which was straight and brown and hung to her shoulders. Looking into the mirror, she tried to see herself as Gigi might be seeing her: a cool kid from a big city who partied and got neat clothes—at a discount. Except for the clothes, this wasn't who she was. And it wasn't who she wanted to be. But at least it was someone who might attract a friend like Gigi. And, at the moment, that's what she needed most—a friend.

Gigi was also in homeroom 3-B, and they sat next to each other. Gigi even introduced her to a few other girls. After the morning announcements, Gigi said, "If you want to meet us at lunch period, we hang out in back of the shed in the school yard."

"What shed?" Angie asked.

"Where they keep the volleyball net and baseball bats and all that stuff. It's a big shed. You can't miss it."

"I'll be there," Angie said. She wasn't looking forward to it too much. She didn't like what "hanging out" might mean. On the other hand, she didn't want to walk into the cafeteria for lunch all alone.

"Behind the shed" meant just what she'd expected. Gigi was there with ten other kids—six girls and four boys. They were passing around a marijuana joint, and several of them were also smoking cigarettes. None of the teachers who patrolled the yard could see what was going on behind the shed unless they came and looked. And, as Gigi explained, the kids took turns standing by the edge of the shed as lookout.

Angie volunteered to act as lookout. But Gigi said, "No! I want you to get to know everyone." She seemed proud to be introducing "Angie-from-the-city, whose dad is the manager at Gardners."

The other kids seemed impressed too. One boy named Joey said, "You probably think we're a bunch of hicks—just smoking pot. I hear that kids in the city use everything. I hear they use pills—and even cocaine."

"Well," Angie said, "mostly the kids in my grade just did pot. Those who did drugs at all."

"There are kids here who don't do drugs," Joey said, "but they're boring. In a town like this there's nothin' else to do. I mean nothin' else worth doing."

"I see," said Angie. Her worst fears about this town were true.

"Yeah," said a girl Gigi had introduced as Sandy. "The other kids call us the 'stoners,' but at least we have fun."

By this time Angie noticed that all the kids—all ten of them— were watching her. And waiting. Waiting for her to toke and pass the joint on. She had never smoked marijuana before in her life. She had never particularly wanted to. The kids she hung out with back home talked about it some; but none of them seemed too set on trying it. Not yet.

The strange thing, she thought, was that these kids didn't seem so different from her friends back in the city. But they were the "stoners." And this wasn't the city. It was Sommerville! Endsville! And she wasn't just 12 any longer. She was almost

13. Angie closed her eyes and toked—not deeply, but deep enough to make her cough. She passed the joint on quickly to Joey. "I've got kind of a cough," she said.

Angie didn't feel any different. All she felt was a kind of disgust. She wouldn't have brushed her teeth with a toothbrush used by all ten of them. But she had just put in her mouth the wet end of a joint they'd all been sucking on.

When it came around to her again, she wondered whether she should say anything about her cough and not wanting to contaminate the rest of them. But as soon as she had the thought, she dismissed it. What she didn't want was to be classified as a nerd, and to these kids that would be about the nerdiest thing she could say. So she toked again. Deeply. And—thank goodness—this time she didn't cough. Also, this time she did feel something. Sort of spacy. A little dizzy. It wasn't a particularly nice feeling.

"It's good stuff, isn't it?" Joey asked, as if wanting the opinion of a big-city expert.

Angie nodded, still unsure of herself.

"You mighta thought we couldn't get good stuff out in the sticks," Sandy said. "But, you see, we can." Angie nodded again. They were all watching her, waiting, it seemed, for her approval. "I see," she said, trying to sound enthusiastic, but somehow the words came out sort of flat.

W hen Angie got home from school that day she found her mother on top of the stepladder, hanging up the living room window drapes.

"You startled me!" her mother said, "I didn't even hear you come in."

Angie dropped her school books on the living room table and plunked herself down on the couch.

"So how was school?" her mother said, coming carefully down from the stepladder.

"Rotten!" said Angie, surprised at the way the word shot out.

Her mother sat on the couch beside her and lit a cigarette.

"You have to expect not to like it for the first few days. But once you make some friends . . . ."

"I made friends," said Angie.

"Well!" Her mother sounded pleased. "That's wonderful, honey. A new girl in a new school in a new town—and you made friends already. You should be very proud of yourself."

"Can I have a cigarette?" said Angie.

"What?" said her mother, looking as though Angie had hit her.

"A cigarette, Mom," Angie repeated. "Kids in school smoke, so why shouldn't I?"

"12- and 13-year-olds smoking cigarettes!" her mother said. "Well, you're certainly not!"

"Why not?" said Angie. "You do. You smoke like a fiend. Dad smokes."

"We'd give anything not to," her mother said. "Cigarettes are so addictive. You know how often we've tried to stop. But we both get so cranky—and I put on weight . . . ." She stubbed

out her cigarette firmly in the ashtray. "Just because I can't seem to stop is no reason you should start. In fact, if I have anything to say about it, you'll never take up this dreadful habit!"

Angie got up. "Well," she said, "I've got some homework to do."

"Did the kids smoke cigarettes in your other school?" her mother asked.

"Sure," said Angie. "Some did."

"How come you never asked me about it before?"

"I don't know," said Angie. She went into her room, closed the door behind her, and stood for a long time looking into the full-length mirror on the back of the closet door. Once again, she tried to see the image of herself that Gigi and Joey and the other kids from the shed might see: a cool kid from the big city. Tears came to her eyes. The image in the mirror began to look wavy and watery. That's who she was, really: this watery shape not knowing what to do. Not knowing who to be. Scared. Scared of being alone. Scared of getting into drugs. Scared of being called a nerd and a creep.

She wiped her eyes. Then she went to her bed and sat down. She sat there for a long time, thinking. Maybe that's what you had to do. See what you were most scared of and deal with that first.

As she left her room, she glanced into the living room. Her mother was on top of the ladder. Quietly, Angie went into the bathroom and closed the door behind her. The medicine chest was filled with bottles. She selected a handful of the most colorful-looking pills and capsules. She could keep them in her purse and have a whole week's supply. Maybe by showing how many pills she had, she could impress people enough so that she could get by without really taking any—or at least without taking many. Pills, she'd heard, were even more sophisticated than marijuana. Well, she'd show them, all right!

Suddenly her mother opened the bathroom door. Angie

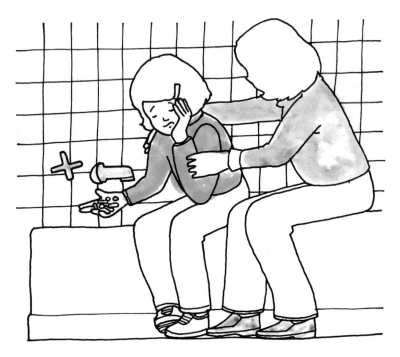

clutched her hand close to her chest, hiding her collection of pills. "What are you doing?" her mother asked.

She stared at her mother. Then suddenly she began to cry. Huge sobs ripped up from deep inside.

"Honey, baby," her mother said. "What is it?" She put her arms around Angie, then sat her down on the edge of the bathtub and sat beside her. Gently, she opened Angie's fist and asked, "What are all these for?" But Angie just kept on sobbing. "Those kids in school," her mother said quietly. "They're doing more than smoking cigarettes, aren't they?"

Angie nodded.

Her mother kept holding her, kissing the top of her head until the sobs quieted. Then her mother spoke gently but firmly. "Stand up." Angie did so. "Throw the pills into the toilet," her mother said. Angie did so. "Flush the toilet," her mother said. Angie obeyed.

"Now," her mother said, "wait right here." She returned with her half-empty pack of cigarettes. One by one, she took the

cigarettes from the pack, tore each one in half, dropped the torn pieces into the toilet, and, finally, flushed them away. "I'm stopping!" she said. "I am never having another cigarette again as long as I live. This time I mean it. On my love for you, Angie, I swear it. If someone offers me a cigarette—I'll just say 'No.' A simple word. It'll be hard to say, but I will say it. 'No thank you. Not for me. Not any more.' And after a while, it'll get easier. People will realize that I'm one of those who doesn't. They'll stop offering me cigarettes. Some people smoke. Some don't. I'll be one of those who don't. And I believe I'll be respected for it."

"I'll respect you, Mom," Angie said softly.

Her mother closed the mirrored medicine cabinet door. Looking into the mirror, they smiled at each other.

The next day in school, it wasn't easy. She kept thinking all through social studies and English how her mother had stood there ripping the cigarettes in half, one by one.

"Just say 'No.' " Her mother's words kept sounding in her head.

Finally it was lunchtime. She and Gigi linked arms as they walked out to the yard and headed over to the shed. Most of the same kids were there. And the same ritual went on. This time Joey was the lookout. A tall, skinny kid named Philip took a joint from the pocket of his plaid shirt and lit it up. He toked deeply and passed it to Gigi, who closed her eyes and inhaled for so long that there was hardly any smoke left to blow out. Then she passed the joint to Angie.

"No, thanks," Angie said.

They all stared at her. Then Philip said, "Maybe you think it's not as good as the weed you get in the city. But it's real good stuff. A few tokes and you'll be flying."

Angie felt her heart thudding. "No, the weed is fine. It's just—I don't understand why you guys have to do everything stoned."

They were still staring at her, as though they weren't hearing right. So she kept on talking into the silence. "Maybe you can deal with everything while you're high. But I can't. I like to remember what I do. I like to keep my head clear."

Philip turned to Gigi, "What's wrong with her?" he said loudly, shaking his head as though he blamed Gigi for what Angie was saying.

Gigi just stared at Angie, her mouth open in disbelief.

"Just because someone doesn't smoke dope doesn't necessarily mean they're a nerd!" Angie said. "They might be perfectly cool."

No one seemed to have anything more to say—including Angie. So she turned and walked away.

She went in to the cafeteria. Alone. But somehow she didn't feel alone. She felt together, with herself.

Star  ters

Why is it so important to make wise decisions about your health? Does it sound like a big responsibility? It is! In order to give yourself a chance to develop your full potential later in life, you need to be making healthy decisions right now. Here are some tips for deciding to become the best and healthiest person you can be:

★ You, and only you, can decide what to make of yourself and your life.

★ Choose to be strong and successful by making healthy and positive decisions for yourself.

★ Stand up for what you believe.

★ Always get the facts before making a decision. Know what you're doing.

★ Be aware that the decisions you make today are shaping the rest of your life.

★ Choose wisely. Choose to be drug-free!

"If you give me a fish, I'll eat for a day. If you teach me to fish, I'll eat for a lifetime."

—Chinese Proverb

Goal Setting

Part 7

"My hopes for the future are to go to a university and to have a good time and have an established career. I think I'll have to work hard on grades and saving money."

"One of my goals now is to be the best head cheerleader that I can be without the whole squad hating me. And to make the squad one of the best we've had in a long time."

"I don't know what I'm going to be. I'm afraid I might fail or disappoint my parents."

"I'd like to change my weight. I'd like to be about ten pounds lighter. I can't do it because I have no will power."

"I would like to change my bad temper. It's like a habit, and it's hard to change."

"I just want to be happy. I don't have any big plan."

"What do I want from life?" "What am I going to be?" These are among the most important questions you can ever ask yourself. If you don't ask these questions, you can end up just drifting through life, like a leaf blown by the winds. On the other hand, you can set goals for yourself and take charge of your life. You can be in control. That's what this section is all about.

W. Clement Stone, one of the most successful businessmen in the United States, is an expert on how to set goals, follow through on a plan, and achieve whatever you set out to do. As he explains in his article titled "Looking Forward: Setting and Achieving Goals," a key ingredient of success is a positive mental attitude. The article offers many different ideas about how you can get to where you want to go in life.

The short story, "Time to Heal," shows how a negative attitude can almost destroy a person. Bobby, the main character in the story, has had a terrible, crippling injury. The only way he'll ever be able to walk normally again is to work hard and keep on hoping. But Bobby finds that hope is in short supply—until one day his mom helps him realize how lucky he is.

Looking Forward: Setting and Achieving Goals

by
W. Clement Stone

T his chapter is dedicated to the most important person in your life: YOU!

In reading this book you've been learning about ways you can make the most of yourself and become the best you can be. All the articles and stories have helped you think about things that are really important, both now and for the rest of your life.

Maybe you've already done some things differently because of what you've read. You've been learning about how to manage your feelings, how to make friends, how to get along with your parents, and how to make healthy decisions. All of these things are important for you to be a successful person. But there's also something else, and that's what this chapter is about. The most successful people are those who learn how to set goals. By thinking about goals—and then following through with action—you can be a success in years to come. You can be the one who makes your future happen.

If you don't set goals, you're really making a decision to do nothing. Every successful person you've met or read about had a Definite Major Goal—every athlete, every entertainer, every great leader in the world.

Do you have a dream for the future? Is it something you're willing to work really hard for? That's what a goal is: something you want very much to do or to be.

To help you think about a goal, answer this question: If you could wave a magic wand and do or be whatever you wanted, what would you wish for? Think about it. That's the first step in setting a goal. You think about where you want to go from here, whether it's tomorrow or five or ten years from now.

Once you think about a goal and write it down, you have taken the first two steps toward achieving your goals.

Some Magic Keys

Wouldn't it be great if you could reach your goals just by wishing? Of course, life doesn't work that way. There aren't any magic wands either. Yet some people don't do anything *except* wish for their dreams to come true.

People who really succeed in life may wish for a little while. We all need dreams. But successful people know that just dreaming isn't enough. They know that to make their dreams come true they need to take action.

In this chapter I'll suggest some things you can do that will help you take action to reach your goals. Think of them as special keys that can open the doors of success for you. They're things you can do to get where you want to go. They worked for me, and they can work for you.

Here's the first one:

Key #1: *Make this promise to yourself: "I will try to learn things that will help me become the best I can be in order to achieve success in everything I do."*

You Can Make Your Dreams Come True

At your age I had big dreams. Each has come true. Even when I was only 12 years old, I knew that I would succeed in business, become wealthy, and marry a wonderful woman. All of those dreams have come true for me. And they can for you too!

Key #2: *Dream big dreams. Set goals for yourself that are really high. As the old saying goes, "The sky's the limit." Aim high!*

Everybody has dreams. So why doesn't everybody achieve success and reach as high as he or she can go? One answer is that life is full of roadblocks. These are things that stand in our way and keep us from achieving our goals.

One roadblock to overcome is fear. Many people fear they will fail or that other people will laugh at them or make fun of them. So they don't try hard, or they give up too easily. I know it's not easy to overcome fear. But you can do it! Let me tell you how I overcame some of the fears that stood in my way.

As a young child, I was very fearful—probably more so than most children. I was so scared during thunderstorms that I ran into the bedroom and hid under the bed. One day while hiding there, I decided that if lightning struck, it would probably be just as dangerous under the bed as anywhere else in the room. So I decided to do away with my fear of lightning. I forced myself to go to the window and look at the flashes of light.

An amazing thing happened: I enjoyed the beauty of the lighted sky and especially the BOOM of the thunder. Today, I really *like* a good, loud storm.

I achieved my goal. That was the beginning of a new habit that has helped me to reach many other goals. I learned how to overcome fear and do what I was afraid to do. This led to one of my favorite sayings: "When you have a worthy goal, do what you're afraid to do. Don't let fear stand in your way."

My Early Childhood

My father died when I was still a young child. Mother and I lived with my aunt and uncle in a rundown neighborhood in the rough, tough South Side of Chicago. Mother worked as a dressmaker. My aunt and uncle waited on tables at restaurants. We were very poor.

As a young boy I wanted to earn money instead of asking my mother for it. So I decided to sell newspapers. You had to buy your papers in advance, and I borrowed the money from a friend. It wasn't much, but it was a lot to me because I didn't have any.

I went to a busy corner—31st Street and Cottage Grove— where two older kids were yelling out the headlines. I tried to act like them and yelled out as loudly as I could. But they turned on me, shouting, "Get out of here!" I refused to leave.

So they beat me up. I was hurt and confused. I cried. I couldn't return the papers. I *had* to sell them.

Not knowing what to do, I walked north on Cottage Grove until I came to Hoelle's Restaurant, which was filled with customers. Since there were so many people, I got an idea. I walked in and sold three papers. Mr. Hoelle kindly pushed me out the door. "That's better than being beaten up," I told myself—and rushed back.

I sold several papers before Mr. Hoelle pushed me out the door again—this time hard and fast. When Mr. Hoelle was some distance from the door, I returned and sold a paper to a customer who liked my attitude and who gave me a dime tip. Mr. Hoelle shoved me out again, even harder than before.

But I walked in again. Then a customer shouted out, "Hoelle, let him alone!" This time he did, and I sold all my papers.

The next evening I returned with twice as many papers. Once again Mr. Hoelle pushed me out the door. But I went right back in, Mr. Hoelle threw his arms up and exclaimed, "What's the use!"

After that Mr. Hoelle and I became good friends. He really helped me and my mother. Times were hard for us, and we were lucky to know him, for he was generous and caring.

I didn't realize until years later that my great successes in the business world had their roots in the many hours I spent as a kid selling newspapers.

Long after I had founded my own company and become a wealthy man, I wrote a book called *The Success System That Never Fails*. As I remembered the days when I worked so hard to sell newspapers, I came up with another key to success. I wrote about it in that book:

Key #3: *To reach your goals you need to have a Positive Mental Attitude. I call it "PMA" for short. With PMA, you can do almost anything. Without it, you may work twice as hard as anyone else and still not succeed.*

How to Develop "PMA"

A positive mental attitude means believing in yourself and your abilities. It means thinking to yourself, "I can do it. Even if it takes a lot of hard work and a long time, I can do it." PMA is like an engine inside you that keeps you going, keeps driving you on.

How do you develop a positive mental attitude? Here are some tips:

- **Start to be more positive.** Some people are always putting themselves down. You may be one of them. Instead of putting yourself down, ask yourself: "What are my good qualities?" (Everybody has some.) "What things do I do best?" "What talents do I have that I can build on?"

- **Take control.** One of the main reasons people don't achieve their goals is that they don't think they have the power to do and get what they want. They always think that someone else is in control. Instead of letting others control you, say to yourself, "I am in control, not someone else. I can succeed if I want to." Make a promise to yourself that you can control at least one bad habit in the next month. An example might be not doing your homework or eating too much candy or junk food. Keep a chart of your progress.

- **Choose friends who you think will help you achieve your goals.** Especially during the teen years, the friends you have influence what you do and think. Ask yourself: "Are my friends the kinds of people who will help me become successful? Do I admire the way they act? Do I admire their goals?"

These are just a few ways you can start to develop a positive mental attitude. They've worked for successful people all over the world.

A Good Example

My mother was one of the most positive people in my life. She had PMA, and she always set a good example for me.

For many years she had worked at Dillon's, one of the best dressmaking companies in Chicago. But she had a Major Definite Goal—to own her own business—and she never forgot that goal.

After only a couple of years at Dillon's, she was completely in charge of all the designing, fitting, and sewing. She was almost as important as the boss himself. She became known for being an outstanding designer and dressmaker.

Her earnings increased every year. And during those years she gave up a lot by saving part of her salary to achieve her goal. Finally, after six years at Dillon's, she opened her own shop in our new apartment in a nice neighborhood. Now she was the boss. She'd reached her goal.

Key #4: Think about the people you look up to. What positive things have they done that you admire?

Some Mistakes in School

After we moved to the nicer neighborhood, I attended public school about six blocks from home. But I wasn't what you'd call a good student. Mostly I got *C*s. I settled for "just passing" instead of trying for high grades.

I didn't know then what I know now. Had I done the work to earn better grades, I would have saved a lot of time and money. Many years later, after I had started my own business, I had to make up for my poor school performance. I had to go to night school so I could learn what I needed to know to pass the entrance exams for a good university.

I did go to a university finally. I had an insurance business—and then many other businesses. I began with only $100 and by working hard, setting goals, and learning about motivation,

I've become a millionaire. Now I'm able to help people all over the world. But I wish I'd had an important key that would have saved me a lot of time:

Key #5: *Don't lose sight of your goal. Keep reminding yourself of what you want to achieve. Take action every day to move in the right direction. Otherwise, you may forget where you want to go.*

Being Open to New Ideas

W hen I was a young teenager, my mother worked very hard in the big city. She believed that it was good for a city boy like me to get out in the country during the summer. But little did she know what an important decision she was making when she sent me to spend a summer at Green's Michigan Farm and Summer Resort.

Exploring the attic one day at Green's Farm, I found at least 50 books written by a man named Horatio Alger. They were dusty and worn, piled neatly in a corner. These books were so popular that millions of kids used to read them, just the way kids watch some popular television shows today. I took one of the books to the front yard, lay in a hammock, and began to read. I was so excited by the stories and the ideas that I read all 50 of the books that summer.

The theme in each book was simple: a young man goes from rags to riches. Each hero was a teenager who was born in poverty but then became a success because:

- He was honest and hard-working.

- He was fair in how he treated other people.

- He did the right thing because it was right.

- He memorized and followed the Golden Rule: Treat others as you would like them to treat you.

The Horatio Alger books inspired me and many other teenagers born in poverty to work to acquire wealth and success the good and right way. Here's another key I learned from reading those 50 books.

Key #6: *Always be open to new ideas. Look for new ways to achieve what you want in everything you read and everything that happens to you. That way, you'll always be moving toward your goals.*

Using Self-Motivators to Get Things Done

If you want to succeed in life, you need to know about setting goals. And you always need to be looking for new information that will help you reach your goals. But none of this will mean very much if you don't put what you know into action.

One way to get things done and take action is to memorize and use self-motivators. These are things you tell yourself that will keep you in action even when you may be feeling that there are too many roadblocks.

Do you ever put things off? Memorizing and applying just three simple words can help you overcome that habit. Repeat the self-motivator "Do it now!" to yourself over and over again when you wake up in the morning and before you go to sleep at night. You'll be amazed how saying these words again and again will keep the words in your mind and help you take action.

Then when you're tempted to put off something important, "Do it now!" will pop into your mind. That's your cue to get into action. With time and practice, you'll find that "Do it now!" will just come to your mind and you'll form a habit of getting things done.

Key #7: Self-motivators can help you reach your goals. Just a few simple words can be your guide to success.

The Most Important Person

Think back for a moment to the words at the beginning of this chapter—"dedicated to the most important person in your life: YOU!"

More and more, as you get older, you'll be the one who's in control of your life. You'll be the one who sets goals, gathers information, figures out a plan, and makes things happen. Think about it. You're the only one who can make you become the best you can be. The time to start is now.

"If you don't know where you're going, you'll end up somewhere else."

Time to Heal

a short story by
Hank Resnik

Bobby should have been working on a book report. Instead he sat in the easy chair with his legs propped up on the footstool, watching TV. Mainly, he was trying not to think about the pain.

His mom came out from the kitchen, where she was finishing the dinner dishes. An apron covered her red skirt and white blouse, the good clothes she wore to her job in an office downtown. With the back of her hand she wiped the dark skin of her forehead. "You want a glass of milk, Bobby?" she asked. "Or how about some fruit juice?"

"Yeah, sure," Bobby said. Then he quickly added, "Please."

His mom turned to go back into the kitchen. "Which do you want— juice or milk?"

"Uh . . . juice, please." But something was bothering him. "Hey, Mom, you don't have to wait on me like in the hospital. I can get it myself."

"Don't be silly," his mom said. "Just relax and I'll get it."

"But I want to do it myself!" Bobby said. He was surprised that suddenly he almost felt like crying.

His mom stood at the kitchen doorway. "I was just trying to do something nice," she said.

Bobby picked up his crutches. With the usual huge effort, which he was beginning to get used to after three days of being home from the hospital, he pulled himself up and started toward the kitchen.

"It's okay," he said as he squeezed past his mother. "See, I can do it myself. Thanks anyway."

After getting a glass of juice, lurching back into the living room, and plopping down in front of the television set again, Bobby closed his eyes. A game show was on. The only reason people watched those shows, he thought to himself, was so they could pretend their wishes were coming true.

With his eyes closed, Bobby thought about his own wish. He wished that the most important moment in his life had never happened—the moment when he'd slid on his skateboard and a car appeared out of nowhere and knocked him down, crushing his left leg. But Bobby knew that wishing wouldn't make a bit of difference. The damage was done.

Dr. Johnson removed the cast exactly eight weeks after the accident. As Bobby sat in the doctor's office and watched the kind old man at work, sawing away at the plaster that covered

the area between the knee and the ankle, he knew this was the beginning of the hard part. And he knew that the hard part might be the rest of his life.

What he knew was that he might never walk again without crutches—or at least a brace on his leg. Bobby, the best back-court shot in the neighborhood. Bobby, the best hitter on the Police Athletic League baseball team. Bobby, who at the age of 13 had already become the star, the leader.

The cast was off now. Where the skin wasn't badly scarred, it was wrinkled and grey, as if it belonged to a dead animal. "Try to move your toes," Dr. Johnson said. Then he waited for a moment. "Well?"

"I'm trying," Bobby said. But nothing happened.

"Try lifting your leg," Dr. Johnson said. "See if you can move it just a little bit."

Bobby closed his eyes and concentrated on moving the leg.

"Hmm," Dr. Johnson said. "Nothing. Try moving just the foot now." But again . . . nothing. Dr. Johnson started to poke at Bobby's leg with what looked like a giant needle. "Feel anything?" Dr. Johnson asked.

"I think so," Bobby said. "Yeah—sort of a tingling."

"Well, that's encouraging," Dr. Johnson said. "It means there's some hope for this leg." He put away the giant needle and rose from his kneeling position. Standing, Dr. Johnson was tall and important-looking. He could have been an African king and his white doctor's coat a king's uniform. But he was kind, and Bobby trusted him.

"In a way, you're lucky," the doctor said. "There's a very slim chance that someday you'll be able to walk normally. For now you'll need crutches. Maybe later on you'll need to wear a brace. You'll also need physical therapy and time, which together might help this leg work better. But we don't know. We just have to try." Dr. Johnson turned to Bobby's mom. "Esther, I'll give you the names of some physical therapists. They'll teach Bobby exercises he can do, and they'll help with regular therapy sessions." Then he turned back to Bobby. "A lot now will depend on you, Bobby. But you've got a great mom to help you, and you're not so bad yourself." Dr. Johnson gave Bobby a friendly slap on the side of his head. Bobby tried to smile.

Bobby's mom smiled too. "I guess I can stand him," she said.

"Well," Dr. Johnson said. "Any questions?"

The three of them were silent. Bobby saw his mom looking at the leg.

"It looks pretty bad right now," Dr. Johnson said. "It'll start looking better. But it's always going to be scarred."

Waiting in the hall for the elevator, Bobby could almost feel his mom trying to think of something positive to say. When she did speak, her voice sounded far away. "Everything's going to be all right," she said.

I̲t was a clear, sunny afternoon. People were sitting on the front steps of apartment buildings talking and laughing, teenagers were dancing on the sidewalks with their radios turned up loud, and younger kids were riding bicycles and skateboards.

Bobby had come home from school on his crutches every day since leaving the hospital. It was only four blocks. But today was different from all the other times. This was his first day without the cast. It didn't make much difference, though. His left leg was as stiff as if it were still covered with plaster. The crutches had become a part of him. They were aluminum, with braces that circled his arms. They were made to last for a long time.

"Hey, Roberto! How's my man?" Bobby turned around at the sound of the familiar voice. It was Mr. Talera, who ran a vegetable market in the middle of the block. For the last two summers, Mr. Talera had let him work as a bag boy. With tips, he could make $20 a week.

"Hi, Mr. Talera, how you doing?" Bobby said.

Mr. Talera had a round face with apple cheeks, and he always seemed to be laughing. "Can't complain," Mr. Talera said. "And you, bambino? You got your cast off? How's that leg?"

"I'm doing all right, Mr. Talera. Thanks." Bobby moved on.

Mr. Talera called after him. "So how long you gotta walk on them crutches? I'm counting on you to help me out again this summer, Roberto. You're one of the best helpers I ever had."

"Maybe you better look for someone else for this summer," Bobby said.

"Aw, go on," Mr. Talera said. "I'm saving the spot for you."

Bobby went on. Turning the corner of his own street, he saw a group of boys sitting on one of the front stoops. Even half a block away, he knew who they were: Tony, Ringo, and Oscar. They were three boys Bobby's age who always hung out together and called themselves the Trouble Brothers. Tony was the ringleader.

As Bobby got closer, the three boys stopped their laughing and joking to stare at him. Bobby stared right back as he passed. But nobody said a word.

Then he heard Tony's voice calling after him. "Hey, Bobby!"

Bobby turned around, steeling himself for whatever came next. Tony kept staring at him. "Yeah?" Bobby said.

"You got your cast off, huh?" Tony asked. Bobby was surprised that the question sounded almost friendly.

"Yeah," Bobby said. "So what?"

"Is it true you're crippled?" Tony asked.

Now Ringo cut in. "Some of the kids were saying you'll never walk without crutches again . . . ."

Even Oscar, who hardly ever talked, had an opinion. "My mom said your leg is ruined," he said. "You'll never do sports or nothing."

"Is it true?" Tony asked.

Bobby could hardly speak. He felt a dull, aching kind of pain he'd never felt before. Finally he spat out an answer. "What happens with my leg is none of your business," he said.

Back in the apartment, Bobby dropped into the easy chair. He rested his legs on the footstool and covered his eyes with his hands.

His mom was in the kitchen, and after a while she came to the doorway. "Hi," she said. "How you doing? Everything okay?"

"Yeah, I guess so."

"What happened?"

"Nothing."

"Nothing—and you're sitting there with your hands over your eyes. Honey, this is your Mama talking."

He dropped his hands and glared at her. "It's not important."

"You went back to school today for the first time without your cast, and nothing important happened. I have a live picture of that!"

"I hate this leg!" Bobby cried. "I hate it!" He swung his arm down on the leg, lying there on the footstool like some dead thing, and hit it as hard as he could with the full force of his fist. "I hate it! Why didn't they cut it off!"

There were tears in his mom's eyes. "Oh Bobby, honey, don't!"

Bobby hit the leg again with his clenched fist—even harder than before. But this time there was a smile on his face. "Hey!" he said. "Whooee! Ma, I think it moved. I could swear it kind of jumped when I hit it. I almost felt like I made it move."

For five minutes Bobby sat there trying to make it move. He thought that if he just wanted it hard enough, it would happen. At one point he even tried hitting the leg again. But it didn't budge.

Finally Bobby sank back in the chair. "Forget it," he said. "It was probably just my imagination. I thought for a second that I made the foot move up. Maybe it didn't happen at all."

"Maybe if you want it enough," his mom said, "it will happen."

"Sure," Bobby said bitterly. "Just like magic."

"I don't believe in magic," his mom said. "But I believe in a few words that can work like magic sometimes. 'Hope.' 'Hard work.' 'Don't give up.' Those words are as good as magic." She stood and looked down at him. "Bobby, I love you very much," she said. "And, I'm telling you, self-pity is a dangerous enemy." For a moment she seemed about to go on with some long lecture. But she stopped. Then all she said was, "I have to get dinner on the table."

It was a Saturday morning. Bobby and his mom were on a bus headed toward the university. He probably would have stayed in bed all morning (unlike the old, energetic Bobby), but she'd made him get up and come with her. He didn't even know where they were going. She said she wanted it to be a surprise.

"Come on," Bobby said at one point. "Tell me. Where are we going?"

His mom just smiled. "You'll see."

He was still puzzled when they got off at the main gate to the university. Then, standing on the sidewalk, he noticed a huge banner hung from the wall next to the gate. It said, "Welcome to the Special Olympics." Crowds of people were passing through the gate.

As they joined the others, Bobby realized that it wasn't like any crowd he'd ever been in. Many of the people looked just like anybody else. But there were clusters of people of all ages, including children and teenagers, all wearing brightly colored athletic uniforms. They seemed to belong to teams. Bobby wondered what kind of teams they could be. Each group had several people who were in wheelchairs. Many were on crutches. Some had heads that seemed larger than normal, or their eyes were an unusual shape.

"What is this?" Bobby said to his mother.

"This is the Special Olympics," she said. "It's like the Olympics, but it's for people with disabilities."

"Oh, great!" Bobby said sarcastically. "This is going to be loads of fun."

She shot him an angry look. "Maybe you'd better not make any prejudiced statements until you've seen some more."

They walked on to the stadium in silence. Inside the stadium they could see that the day's events had already begun. As they sat down, a gun went off, signaling the beginning of a wheelchair race. About a dozen people in wheelchairs raced through a series of red cones at one end of a track. When they reached the finish line, everybody in the race was showered with kisses and hugs from people who were cheering them on. Bobby could hardly believe his eyes. He'd never seen so many people hugging each other. Even in the stadium itself, the spectators seemed to bubble over with friendliness. The crowd cheered louder than any crowd that Bobby had ever heard—and kept cheering until the last wheelchair had crossed the finish line.

"Everyone who participates receives a medal," Bobby's mom said. "The whole idea is that everyone is a winner. See that banner?" She pointed to the stands opposite, where a huge banner hung. On it were the words, "Let me win, but if I cannot win, let me be brave in the attempt."

As Bobby was taking all this in, another gun went off, and the voice coming over the loudspeaker announced that it was the beginning of a series of 200-meter races. A group of young people could be seen running around the track. Most of them were teenagers. To Bobby they looked fairly normal.

As before, the crowd continued to clap and cheer for all of the athletes. Bobby wondered why the clapping and cheering continued even after the last runner had crossed the finish line. But then he realized that the one he'd thought was last wasn't last at all. He just hadn't noticed a runner who was far behind the main group. And he was far behind because he was running on crutches. It seemed to Bobby as if a great wave of clapping and cheering followed this lonely runner on crutches all the way to the finish line.

Bobby and his mom watched the Special Olympics for several hours, and in all that time they hardly spoke. There was an occasional "Did you see that?" or "Wow—look at that!" but not much else.

In the bus going home, Bobby's head was crowded with thoughts. He'd never felt this way before, and he knew that somehow, for some reason, his life would never be the same again.

As they neared their own apartment building, Bobby realized what time it was. "Hey," he said to his mom. "If I don't hurry I'm going to be late for my physical therapy session. And I'd better get there. I've got a lot of work to do."

His mom's eyes opened wide. "You do?"

Bobby smiled. "Are you kidding? Of course! If the people I saw today can do the things they do against those odds, so can I! I may even make this old leg run again. I've got so much work to do it's incredible!"

His mom reached out and brushed his head with her hand. "I don't know," she said. "You've come pretty far already."

Bobby grabbed her hand. "You watch, Mama," he said. "You haven't seen anything yet." Then he paused for a moment and looked straight into her eyes. "Thank you, Mama," he said. "Thanks for everything."

Star  ters

The key to being successful in life is to decide on goals and then start to make them happen. Remember these points as you go for your goals:

★ First, you have to have a dream—destinations in mind.

★ Make your dreams into goals.

★ Plan each step of what you need to do to reach your goals. Then take one step at a time.

★ Obstacles are challenges—don't let them stop you.

★ Keep moving in the right direction and you'll get there.

About the Authors

Gary R. Collins is a clinical psychologist, a psychology teacher, and an internationally known authority on early adolescence. He has written nearly 30 books, including one dealing with teenage stress entitled *Give Me a Break.* He is also the author of *The Joy of Caring* and *You Can Profit from Stress.* He works with teenagers every day and consulted with many teenagers in writing the chapter for this book. He and his wife are parents of two teenagers who made it successfully through the junior high school years.

Dr. Bill Cosby is respected as an entertainer throughout the world. He has appeared in several major television shows and series and is best known for his most recent series, "The Cosby Show." Because of his interest in young people, he took time off from his work as an entertainer to get a doctoral degree in education from the University of Massachusetts. He continues to be involved in a variety of youth-oriented programs, and he is the father of five children.

Rick Little became nationally known as a leader in programs for youth before he finished college. He inspires thousands of teenagers with a practical, warm, and understanding message, and he makes presentations to young people and educators throughout the United States and other countries. He has also appeared widely on television talk shows with his message of positive youth development. Rick is the founder and president of Quest International and has personally helped to implement positive programs for youth in hundreds of schools and communities.

Peggy Mann has written more articles for the general public on the health hazards of marijuana than any other writer in the world. Since 1978 she has specialized in writing articles on marijuana, on drug abuse among youth, and on alcohol, drugs, and driving. She writes regularly for the *Reader's Digest,* and one of her articles for that magazine on the drug problem has been among the *Digest's* most frequently requested reprints. She is also well known for her more than 30 books for young readers. Her latest book, published by McGraw-Hill, is *Marijuana Alert.*

Hank Resnik has written many articles and books for and about young people and is one of the country's leading writers on topics related to youth and education. He has contributed to many national magazines, including *Saturday Review, The Atlantic,* and *Redbook.* His most recent book, co-authored for the National Institute on Drug Abuse, is *Teens in Action,* which consists of profiles of a variety of teenagers across the country who have helped make it easier for other teenagers to say "No" to alcohol and drugs.

Charlie W. Shedd is a husband, father, and best-selling youth author. As a regular columnist for *Teen Magazine,* he has received more than 25,000 letters from teenagers across America telling about their problems and looking for his help. His books sell by the millions and charm kids and parents alike. *Letters to Karen, Letters to Philip,* and *The Stork is Dead* are just a few of his well-known best-sellers.

W. Clement Stone is an internationally renowned philanthropist, civic leader, author, publisher, businessman, and Nobel Peace Prize nominee. His philosophy that everyone is capable of success, "no matter how poor his start in life," is carried to millions through his speeches, magazine articles, and self-help books such as *Success Through a Positive Mental Attitude* and *A Success System That Never Fails.* It has also helped to form the basis of a multi-million-dollar business that has allowed him to support many important humanitarian causes. His interest in young people led him to offer major support, through the W. Clement and Jessie V. Stone Foundation, to the Lions-Quest *Skills for Adolescence* program.

Barbara Varenhorst is a former junior high school English and social studies teacher and counselor. She is the director of the Peer Counseling Program in Palo Alto, California, which pioneered the concept of peer counseling and remains one of the best-known programs of its kind in the country. She is a frequent consultant to school districts, and she is also the author of a book for teenagers titled *Real Friends* (Harper & Row, 1983). Her regular contact with teenagers served as the basis for her observations about teenagers and friendship in this book.

A Note About the
Skills for Adolescence
Program and
Quest International

This book is part of *Skills for Adolescence,* a joint program of Lions Clubs International and Quest International. The program offers a complete set of lessons for a course that helps to teach young adolescents (10-14-year-olds) skills they will need for healthy growth and positive decisions. In addition to this book, the program provides a detailed, step-by-step teacher's manual for implementing the course, a student workbook, a student notebook for personal reflections, and a book for parents on issues of early adolescence. The program includes intensive teacher training, parent involvement in many of the lessons and activities, and a series of parent meetings on ways of coping with issues of early adolescence and improving family communication.

Each of the articles and stories in this book corresponds to a specific lesson in the curriculum manual that contains questions and points for discussion. The seven parts of the book correspond directly to the seven units of the curriculum:

Unit One: *Entering the Teen Years: The Challenge Ahead*

Unit Two: *Building Self-confidence Through Better Communication*

Quest International is a nonprofit organization founded in 1975 that specializes in programs for positive youth development. In addition to *Skills for Adolescence,* Quest has developed *Skills for Living,* a semester course in positive life skills for students in grades 10-12, and *Project LEAD,* a program created in collaboration with the Association of Junior Leagues that promotes youth involvement in projects to improve schools and communities through service learning. Quest International is also a founding member of the National Coalition for the Prevention of Drug and Alcohol Abuse and is funded by dozens of foundations, corporations, and contributions from those who support its work with young people. For more information contact Quest International, 537 Jones Road, P.O. Box 566, Granville, Ohio 43023-0566. Or call 614/587–2800.

STAFF

Quest International
  Vice President for
    Program Development:
    Susan Carroll Keister

Editors:
    Linda Barr
    Marba Wojcicki

Managing Editor:
    Richard Kinsley

Proofreader:
    Peg Williams

Assistants:
    Deborah German
    Deborah Washington

Art Director and
  Production Supervisor:
    LeRoy Wittemire

Illustrations:
    Don Robison

Photos: Pages 28, 78. **Edmonton, Alberta, Board of Education.** Pages 2, 80, 116. **Frank Espada.** Cover. **Bill Gill.** Pages 12, 39, 64, 138, 144, 170, **Larry Hammill.** Page 107. **Ted Rice.** Pages 10, 34, 58, 86, 90, 109, 111, 161, 167. **David S. Strickler.** Page 131. **Youth to Youth.**